W. Lawrence Lipton

presents

The Tea Party
America Upended
The Elections 2014 & 2016

W. Lawrence Lipton

presents

The Tea Party

Upending America
The 2014 & 2016 Elections

Copyright © 2014

Books may be ordered through booksellers or by contacting:

www.createspace.com/4617610
www.Amazon.com

———————

CreateSpace Title ID: <4617610>

Jacked Design by Guebres Studios

ISBN-13: 978-1494996499 (sc)
ISBN-10: 1494996499 (ebk)

Printed in the United States of America
CreateSpace date: 01/15/2014

Think About This

To those who would change America.
This is your time in history.
To encourage a thing,
First lie about it;
Then prohibit it.

BUT

"And if a house be divided against itself,
that house cannot stand. {*Mark 3:25*}
as utilized by
'*Common Sense*', Thomas Paine, 1776;
Sam Houston, 1850; Abe Lincoln, 1858

"... and upon that foundation
do our enemies build
their hopes of subduing us."
Abigail Adams, c.1812

"In the world's greatest deliberative body,
no one is listening."
'*The Audacity of Hope*', Barack Obama, 2006

"nobody knows anything"
Said of Hollywood by William Goldman,
"*Adventures in the Screen Trade*", 1983

CHAPTERS

Prologue

Those who have read, or have tried to read, my more recent books know I am happy to set the record straight, but have no reason to insist people learn, or behave in the own best interest. I concluded the first paragraph of *'Saint Paul's Joke'*, by stating, "if you are absolutely certain that your perspective on the Gospels is correct, and, within your mind will allow no possibility that you are wrong, and are willing to bet everything on that, it is unlikely you will want to read further." We can apply the same statement to the Tea Party.

Why would an author, one who specializes in an analytical analysis of major cultural constants, seek to have people avoid reading his work?

After all, wouldn't it be much easier just to NOT write and publish the observations – or to publish in some obscure academic journal and hope that nobody cites what you have revealed?

The information must be made available, it must be easily accessible to whoever has an honest interest in it. But, it should not be thrust upon those who would live their lives in ignorance.

Well, there is the rub. Publishing in an academic journal has always carried the real risk of a finding being quoted, then wending its way into the mainstream media, altering any predictions. In reality, the idea is to be on record – without altering history.

A Brit named Douglas Adams wrote *'The Hitchhiker's Guide to the Galaxy,'* in which the main character, Arthur Dent, awakens to discover his home is about to be demolished to make way for a highway bypass; the story progresses very quickly to the point where we learn, unbeknownst to him, his best friend is an alien, and the earth is about to be demolished to make way for a hyperspace bypass.

In each instance, the demolition crew foreman, respectively, chides Dent and the people for complaining when all the relevant plans had been properly posted for comment – Arthur's were on the bulletin in the City Hall basement, and the Earth's at an equivalent location in Alpha Centori. Clearly, it isn't the foreman's problem if they can't take a proper interest in regional affairs.

As we all know, there is a class of people who routinely hold-up, or cite, the Bible as the basis of their beliefs. Yet they have never actually read the Book, or, if they have, never took the trouble to understand its words in the context in which they were delivered.

Almost no one knows that the Christian Calendar, which has become our modern western calendar, is actually a continuation of the ancient Hebrew Calendar – as I explained in my book '*Genesis of Genesis*'. A fact for which we can thank a Scythian monk call Dennis the Small – who, in our year 525AD, is said to have fixed his year one relative to "the incarnation of our Lord Jesus Christ," but, in fact, simply reset to one at a primary Hebrew celebration node which is now known as a metonic cycle upon which both the Hebrew and Chinese calendar systems are based.

Of course nobody is interested in that, or why Genesis Patriarchs have such long lifespans. Facts seldom trump belief and superstition, as some of you have seen (Pope Benedict prior to his retirement decision) and then acted upon, even the letters of Saul of Tarsus – known today as Saint Paul – have been replaced with Roman superstition.

As shown in '*Saint Paul's Joke*', it is no wonder that Jesus himself declared there would be those who would claim to come in his name, but he wouldn't know them, and certainly would not be the one to argue their case Judgement Day. But then, who has ever asked why the scriptures declare 144,000 Jews get a free pass – but, in a Christian canonical prophecy, not a single 'Christian' is assured automatic salvation. It's what I chose to call '*Saint Paul's Joke*'.

But what has this to do with The Tea Party and the future of America? And why would anyone listen to the ranting of a baptized Irish Catholic, Bar Mitzvah German Jew, whose been a Democratic County Chairman who publically supported Republican Senatorial candidates over his own party's nominees – and, given their record in office, was never given cause to regret that decision?

See. I'm doing it again. I'm giving the dullards among you cause not to read further, and so entrapping you – making you responsible for not dealing with the reality which will result from the you electing the people who seek to destroy our nation. The true beauty of it all? You don't even know who, or what, the candidates represent – and they are very careful to keep it that way.

Who are The Tea Party?

Who represents them and stands as their leadership?

Officially, The Tea Party is not a registered national political party, and neither "The Tea Party" nor the "Tea Party Movement" can appear in association with a candidate's name on any ballots.

Depending on your politics, you might compare The Tea Party to a Resistance Movement, or a terrorist organization. In either case, The Tea Party is actually a network of loosely organized and generally uncoordinated cells which profess their adherence to a vaguely worded ten point agenda, or platform.

One website proclaims The Tea Party to be "essentially a populist movement urging political change for the benefit of the people. The focus is on fiscal conservatism." The it goes on to associate the Party with the conservative and libertarian goals of decreased taxation and spending. [www.what-is-the-tea-party.com]

So, when we ask who they are, and who their leadership is, the answer can only be given in an inaccurate and vague manner of asserted goals without a formal leadership structure. But it is a real movement, and a failed activist history.

On 27 February 2009 it had its first 'major' protest – against the Troubled Assets Relief Program (TARP) which, the previous year, had been signed into law by Republican President George W. Bush. Ten days after it was signed into law by President Barack Obama, they protested against another Bush program – American Recovery and Reinvestment Act (ARRA).

In both instances, the retroactively protested laws were perceived to be bailouts of those who had caused the 2007 recession and mandated the newly elected Obama spend at levels which would increase the both the Deficit and National Debt.

As did many al-Qaeda groups, Tea Party members formally commemorated the first anniversary of the September 11 terrorist attacks on the United States. The events of 9/11 had underscored the failure of Republican defense and security protocols which had formed a centerpiece of GOP politics since the Reagan Era. The failure of Bush's 'War on Terror' – marked by administration lies about Iraqi WMD's, and a failure to apprehend, or kill the boastful architect of 9/11, Osama Bin Laden – served to further underscore Republican military incompetence and wastefulness.

On 14 March 2010, The Tea Party launched a protest again the Patient Protection and Affordable Care Act – now widely known as Obamacare. Their ten day protest ended with President Obama signing the Act into law on the 23rd of March.

As the principal health policy adviser under President George H. W. Bush, Republican Tom Scully, revealed, "Obamacare, was largely based on past Republican initiatives. If you took [Bush's] health plan and removed the label, you'd think it was Obamacare."

Under George W. Bush, Scully ran the Centers for Medicare and Medicaid Services and oversaw a host of proto-Obamacare reforms, like Medicare Part D, which introduced competition into the government-supported health care market.

Republican initiatives – like the shift to a private-insurance program – were also formulated by Scully and other Republicans with the objective of reducing state costs by billions of dollars, and it appears that this marks a rare Republican cost cutting success.

We would note that the Affordable Care Act is not a single payer socialist program. Rather is is a free market, private sector controlled, program which was originally proposed by Republican Conservative Ronald Reagan; having failed to gain Congressional support, the program was revamped under President George H. W. Bush; it was again revamped, and, as Scully noted, achieved its current form under President George W. Bush. All of which served to make Obamacare an example of a Compassionate Conservative free market approach to the critical American Health care issue.

The opposition to Obamacare evidences a persistent pattern of Tea Party attacks upon Republican programs and initiatives designed to indemnify, or enrich, greedy capitalist monopolies.

If, as our basis, we utilized the attacks on Obamacare – and the October 2013 governmental shutdown which resulted from a failed effort to defund a health care program which had been law for almost three years, than we could assert that Republican Senator Ted Cruz of Texas was among the upper echelon leaders within a group which boasts no formal leadership.

Reality dictates that Senator Cruz be seen to represent the political equivalent of a suicide bomber – one whose actions are both dramatic and pointless, but which inflict hardship on innocent third parties. As we know, the sixteen day governmental

shutdown October involve makes a big show of engaging in a destructive action which threatens the lives of innocents, but achieves very little in the way of substance.

The Tea Party would have you think of them as a grassroots movement – one built on the backing of the proletariat – which will spawn an awareness of issues which challenge American security, sovereignty or domestic tranquility.

The Tea Party is not intended to initiate affirmative action; it does not offer solutions; nor does it clearly define the nature of the problem. Its primary purpose is opposition. As with any good resistance group, in a time of war, The Tea Party serves to disrupt and hamper the progress of targeted 'occupying army', and it can be found within the occupied territory – in the current instance, this is the ranks of the Republican Party.

As with any Resistence Movement, its ranks contain those who define, and therefore oppose, any 'foreign force' as the enemy. As a result, they can be seen to attack their potential allies, as well as the defined enemy.

These attacks are generally counterproductive, often taking the form of suicidal actions, accompanied by an assertion of obvious falsehoods, and a demonstrative distortion of reality.

Who are The Tea Party – who represents their rank and file?

Apparently, various surveys and poles present an image of a Tea Party movement which is equally represented by females and males who are predominantly white, married, over the age of 45 and roughly half are born-again Christian.

They tend to be conservative, and therefore more favorable

to Republicans than Democrats. They are also more educated and have more accumulated wealth than the general population.

On some levels, one could hold that the Tea Party movement is composed of traditional Republicans who are simply engaged in a process of rebranding traditional GOP policies and candidates by restating those traditional policies while holding that the Reagan Era presentation has failed, or was wrongheaded – hence the attack on the Reagan program which evolved and eventually became law as the Affordable Care Act, and is denounced as Obamacare.

Part of the rebranding process involves disavowal of any and all connections to programs which originated in the Reagan Era. If we look closely, the idea of "tax and Spend" represents the process associated with a balanced budget; and the Reagan conservative ideal focused on continuing"borrow and spend" policies. Therefore we can objectively observe that the National Debt doubled under Reagan; was on the way to doubling under President George H. W. Bush (a process stopped by his being voted out of office); then, once again doubled under President George W. Bush.

If we wished to see fiscal conservatives, we would need to look at the record for President Bill Clinton, and – despite the fact the 2007 recession caused by George W. Bush put upward pressure on the Deficit and National Debt – spending under Barack Obama has still moved in the direction of deficit and debt reduction.

On February 19, 2009, a week before TARP demonstration, CNBC commentator Rick Santelli had referenced the Boston Tea Party (1773) as part of his denouncement of the government bailout which only served to "subsidize the losers' mortgages" – he then went on to propose a Chicago Tea Party to protest any intervention in the burst housing market bubble. Thus the established origins of the Tea Party Movement can be traced to a commentator, speaking in reaction to, rather than warning of, an economic disaster which was, in fact, a demographic necessity.

Standing in the wings of the show was an emerging racist response to the November 2008 election of Barack Obama, coupled to the obvious failures of yet another Republican administration.

Anti-Republican

The joint reaction to the Compassionate Conservative Free Market Republican legislation – now known as Obamacare – and election of Barack Obama, takes the form of discussion group posts which lack both substance and civility – posts like this one:

"Like I said, Assbama is a lying, tyrant and PUNK-ASS-BITCH. Nothing more. He is EVIL. I feel very sorry for those of you who believe in him. He has nothing to offer but OUR money. Not his. He will be punished for that in the future. He should be arrested, tried, convicted and EXECUTE, NOW. PERIOD, PERIOD and PERIOD. Like the little bastard said, if you want it you can keep it. WELL, I say, if you want him, you can shove him up your butts. JUNK THE PUNK, NOW. Also, his wife, the BEASTY ONE can go too. I am SPARKY1845"

If we use the internet news forum discussion group pages as our criteria, than this is represents the intellectual and educational level of the average Tea Party demographic.

There is obviously a vehemence which can only be expressed in childish word plays on the President's name; name calling; the accusation of evil which, by reference to the statement "if you like you policy, you can keep it" infers that universal health care is evil; there is even a gratuitous insult tossed at the First Lady. Yet we can see that nowhere is there anything factual, tangible, or concrete to justify the obvious anger.

Is the President – more accurately, is Congress using "our money," rather than theirs? Of Course. That is their job, and the money they use are the taxes we pay. Has a crime been committed? If so, is that crime derived from the requirement that individuals carry insurance? If it is, then every state mandating automobile coverage has legislatures which are also guilty of a crime. Drivers do not plan on, intend to, being in an accident, nor do people plan on suffering from some catastrophic medical problem – yet we know it happens.

Setting aside the obvious factual ignorance, the style is one which has become all too common across the internet

As of December 2013, *Google* and the *Huffington Post* were in the process of restoring civility to their discussions– in part by deploying moderators, and rejecting screen names, so people would need to use their real names and take personal responsibility for any comments like that presented here (and all too common among Tea Party supporters).   With any luck, these efforts will restore civil discourse on online comment threads, and introduce thought-out intelligence to the Internet wastelands.

One can make an argument for anonymity. It does allow for speech without repercussion, but that means hate speech abounds and tends to drown out the whistle blowers and those who have a legitimate basis for protest, or to espouse unpopular opinion. The real issue that intelligent discussion is suppressed by those who are dishonest – bigoted trolls, or bullies are given free license to pick arguments, threaten and abuse.

Think about some of the more popular dishonesty which has emerged around Barack Obama and a generalized comment of the type SPARKY1845 demonstrated –"lying, tyrant and PUNK-ASS-BITCH. ... evil." Yet the House fails to generate an impeachment.

Impeachment would be the natural course, if the assertions that Obama was not Constitutionally eligible to be President had any merit – there is a claim that, like his father, Obama was born in Kenya, rather than Hawaii (two years after it acquired statehood). But they ignore the small things, like the fact that the hospital provided the birth record to the Department of Health – along with all the other births during that period in 1961. Then too there is the matter of the Department of Health tabulating the recorded births and issuing a complete list of all the recorded births – which was subsequently published by the Honolulu newspapers.

"Birthers," as they are called, habitually dispute documents of the type routinely supplied in response to requests for certified copies of birth certificates – but they carefully avoid addressing the issue of the published record of all births, or the lack of immigration records which would establish that Obama's mother, Stanley Ann Dunham Obama, was out of the country on the 4th of August 1961.

Clearly, showing the Immigration and Naturalization record for the border crossing by his mother – either via American, or British-Kenyan port of entry records – would be far more valid than alleged 'expert opinion' that a recently generated certified copy of an archived record is 'imperfect.' After all, if his mother was not in Honolulu's Kapi'olani Maternity & Gynecological Hospital – if she was not even in the country – on the day he was born, then he could not have been born in America.

Of course, were that shown, that also raises other questions.

If he was born outside America, who falsified the birth record so that his name would be in the newspaper listing of births? The next lie, and fraud, to be asserted would be that the immigration records in both American and Britain (Kenya had not yet been given its Commonwealth independence) were falsified.

Interestingly, since he had traveled to Indonesia as a child, that falsification had to be prior to acquiring an American Passport; which means it had to be done when Obama was a five or six years old – his age when he, his mother and step-father were living in Jakarta.

Among rational, intelligent, people, there is a commonly held, deep rooted, necessity to reconcile facts to support, or refute, assertions. That trait is missing among people like SPARKY1845; it is also missing among born-again Christian ministers like Rafael Cruz, father of Senator Rafael Edward 'Ted' Cruz – both of whom are discussed in my 2013 book, "*President Ted Cruz*."

After he gained national attention with his twenty-one hour quasi-filibuster, Ted Cruz was mentioned in terms of repeating the political path taken by Obama – that is, running for President.

In August 2013, Ted Cruz stated: "Now the Dallas Morning News says that I may technically have dual citizenship. Assuming that is true, then sure, I will renounce any Canadian citizenship. Nothing against Canada, but I'm an American by birth and as a U.S. senator; I believe I should be only an American."

Note, the man is a Harvard educated attorney – top in his class – and, in 1986, presented a birth certificate establishing he was natural born Canadian and received his American Passport.

Yet he still asserts he is an "American by birth." A statement which best befits one who expects to be a Presidential Nominee in 2016, or a some point thereafter. Yet it is a statement which can only be considered 'factually accurate' if he is lumping Canada and the United States together under the geographic use of "America."

The problems which arise are multi-faceted.

We can set aside the classic 'Lawyer's Lie' about being born in the Americas, or in a country on the north American Continent, and focus on a factual comparison to Obama.

Remember, in order to travel to Indonesia when he was five, Barack Obama would have had to have had a passport, and that would have required a birth certificate and documentation which would have come forward with each and every subsequent passport.

Thus, Obama's original passport would have indicated that either Hawaii, or Kenya, was his place of birth. Therefore, asserting Obama was born in Kenya, when his documents state Hawaii, is to say that Obama would have had no knowledge of his place of birth – therefore would not be a lair if he claimed citizenship via being a Hawaiian by birth.

However, that said, there appears to be a reason for people asserting that Barack was born in Kenya – in 1991, Obama's Literary Agent issued a pamphlet in which he gave brief biographies of his clients. In it he made a erroneous statement about Obama: 'Born in Kenya and raised in Indonesia and Hawaii.'

If that statement was not erroneous, than the Republican leadership was willful negligent in its responsibility to challenge Obama's nomination; it then compounded that incompetence by failing to challenge the election results, and further underscored its lack of competence through a failure of the House leadership to institute requisite impeachment proceedings in accordance with the eligibility clause of the Constitution.

Article II, Section 1, of the Constitution states: *"No Person except a natural born Citizen, or a Citizen of the United States, at the time of the Adoption of this Constitution, shall be eligible to the Office of President; neither shall any Person be eligible to that Office who shall not have attained to the Age of thirty five Years, and been fourteen Years a Resident within the United States."*

Neither Obama nor Cruz – nor anyone alive today – could have been citizens when the Constitution was adopted (September 17, 1787), thus rendering that qualification null and void.

Thus the issue falls on the meaning of the words, *"natural born Citizen,"* words which cannot be altered by simple legislation.

If the Supreme Court, or an Amendment to the Constitution, were to define that term as "any individual, regardless of place of birth, has one American parent," then both Obama and Cruz are, by virtue of their respective mothers, equally qualified

In contrast, if Ted Cruz had ever gotten a passport, or any government document which required a place of birth (and possibly citizenship), Canada would have clearly appeared along with the nature of his American citizenship. So, unless Cruz can show that there is no mention of his Canadian birth on any of his documents, it becomes clear that he knowingly lied in his August statement.

The ball is in the 'Birther" court, will they attack candidate Ted Cruz in the same way they have attacked Obama, or will they reveal themselves to be willfully hypocritical? Of course they might escape such revelations – Ted Cruz might follow the suggestion made in *"President Ted Cruz"* and declare himself ineligible to run for either President or Vice-President.

Cruz's documents branding him responsible for any deceit that can be associated with his August statement. But, if there was any deception on the part of Obama, it had to be perpetrated, at the time of his birth, by either his grandparents or parents – and it had to be in collusion with someone either at the Kapi'olani Hospital, or in the Honolulu Department of Health.

An infant cannot forge the documents necessary to obtain a passport or birth announcement (with associated official records), so Obama has done nothing. Nor can we hold him liable for false assertions by a literary agent in a brochure associated with a book which was never published.

But how do we defend Cruz? He must take full responsibility for his deceit.

As for The Tea Party, or Tea Party Movement. Since their organizers, sponsors, or promoters, have been careful to establish they are not a formal organization, there is no specific individual, or board of governors, who can be held liable for anything asserted by those who wish to operate under a Tea Party moniker.

The same problem emerges when we talk of '*Birthers.*'

Essentially, both the Tea Party and 'Birther' Movement are code names for individuals who are hypocritical and intellectually dishonest. There the elected Representatives in Congress have no reason to act upon the type of random generalizations whose extreme elements are represented by various 'Talk Show" types of the type which pander to individuals like SPARKY1845.

Without question, The Tea Party Movement is a challenge to the old guard Ronald Reagan Republican Conservative Party – but without a "Voice." There is no "Ronald Reagan" to take the helm and guide it into the new century.

The old guard had to pass. There is no doubt about that. The Marxist Socialist Communist "enemy" has become a New Capitalist Master. Russia has become a diplomatic Allie; Red China is now our biggest creditor; both economies are rapidly growing and are easily on track to surpass the American Capitalist Dream.

Granted, both of those socialist economies have exhibited their version of growing pains, but they are still on track to be the type of socialist nation we see throughout the Scandinavian region.

Western knee-jerk reactions to all things labeled 'socialist' has crashed headlong into the concept of basic Christian Values and the specific teachings associated with Jesus and Paul. No longer can we claim to be a Christian Nation and deny Christian Values by imparting them with the "socialist" label. We must confront the fact that, be we Christian or Jew, we are bound by Law of Reciprocity – by the '*Golden Rule*' – to treat others as if they were us, to do for them what we would hope they would do for us, if we were in their current circumstances.

The Reagan Era paradigm was defined in the narrow terms of absolutes: Black & White; Socialist vs Capitalist; Them & Us; 'traditional' (1950's *Leave It To Beaver*') families; Male & Female Roles, Responsibilities, or Careers. None of those paradigms have a functional place in modern society.

Where we were faced with organized armies and a Cold War in which the armies tested each other in out-of-the-way countries – these have given way to well financed suicidal non-State related terrorist organizations.

In response to suicidal criminals and murders destroying the World Trade Center, and attempting to destroy the Pentagon, we declared a "War on Terror" in which there was no defined enemy, nobody who could surrender, or sign an armistice. Our President, George Bush, even went so far as to declare the architect of 9/11 to be 'irrelevant' in our "War on Terror."

If it had been the Reagan Era, or, better, the Roosevelt Era of 1941, would we have tolerated a President who said Hitler was irrelevant?

Is the modern paradigm one in which we lash out without a plan or concrete objective? Is this the "War on ____" era in which the war is one of attrition and there is no enemy leadership authorized to end the conflict? Declare a "war on drugs," or a "war on terror," maybe a 'war on stupidity' which will wipe out those who promoted the first two wars? In October 2013 we had a government shutdown which threatened the reliability of American lawful debt – it was a war in retaliation for losing the same repeal vote 42 times.

Those who declared the war never explained: Why is it bad for private insurers to insure more people – so the government does have to face the choice between paying the cost of chronic illness, or having voters enraged because grandma, or babies, are dying for want of medical treatment? We want the babies to be born, not aborted, but we refuse to pay for the medical care that will see them born healthy, but which mama can't afford?

Let's Eliminate?

Though it has no formal structure, no defined leadership, it appears the Tea Party Movement does have roughly defined Ten Point Platform, which begins with the idea we need to Eliminate.

The first three items on the Ten Point political agenda are:

1. Eliminate Excessive Taxes - Excessively high taxes are a burden for those exercising their personal liberty to work hard and prosper as afforded by the Constitution. A fiscally responsible government protects the freedom of its citizens to enjoy the fruits of their own labor without interference from a government that has exceeded its necessary size, scope and reach into the lives of its citizens.

2. Eliminate the National Debt - By implementing fiscally conservative policies at all levels of government, progress can be made toward eliminating the U.S. National Debt. Massive increases in the National Debt have created and continue to create a huge burden for the next generation of Americans, thus imperiling the country's short-term and long-term economic health and prosperity.

3. Eliminate Deficit Spending - All deficit spending must be eliminated immediately. We insist that government representatives at all levels maintain a fiscally responsible budget and balance the books as would be expected of any American business.

How do we "eliminate" any of these interconnected economic woes, without a major alteration our economic thinking?

Our Constitution decrees that all lawful debts must be paid. The National debt must be paid; we borrow money to cover deficit spending; deficits arise when expenses exceed revenues – and for governments, revenues are represented by taxes and fees. We pay tolls to cover the cost of our interstate highways and on various bridges or tunnels; thus the cost, the associated debit incurred to construct them, is covered by those who use them. There are also commerce taxes – Value Added Tax (VAT), Service and Sales Taxes – which are also use taxes, paid by those who select to purchase a given product or service.

For local communities, the cost of maintenance is not a toll, but an annual property tax paid by full and part-time residents.

At what point do these various taxes become excessive?

Should taxes designate for education – Local School Taxes – be 'use taxes' and paid only by those who have children in the public system. It would certainly be more equitable for those who choose to send their children to private schools. And definitely fairer to those who chose not to have children – after all, why should they pay to educate their neighbor's il-mannered brat?

Maybe we should consider returning to that pre-1913 era when eight years of education was considered more than sufficient for the average person. Why should people without children fund High School, possibly even University, educations?

Clearly the "Right-To-Life" groups would have no trouble supporting a tax on those who have children – they already want to impose a range of costs because of defective birth control measures; people who then selected to abort the unplanned for, unwanted, fetus, so what's one more tax/cost?

We already know that the "Right-To-Life" groups do not see their 'moral' position as the imposition of a tax, but, in practicality, that is exactly what they are doing, creating an excessive user tax on someone who doesn't want the product.

There was a time, prior to 1913, when property taxes were the Constitutional basis for most government revenues. But, when the relationship between income and property became disconnected – when the majority of income was earned by those who felt no need to own physical property; when a actor in the new silent movies could earn more in a week than the average worker could hope to earn in an year, when people began getting rich off their ideas, their thoughts, their stories, because they owned the patent or copyright, the Constitutional tax structure was easily avoided, or evaded.

We forget that it was only after 1913 that there was a move to encourage people to own their own homes. Prior to 1913, many immigrants ran businesses from their rented apartments, they did piecework in their kitchen. We need only search the Internet to find old photographs of families, or small groups of individuals, sitting at a kitchen table and earning a piecework garment industry living.

One of my own grandfathers, when he immigrated to New York, earned his income doing piecework at his brother's kitchen table. For his first fifteen years in America, he didn't need to pay taxes – not was he expected to. Should we return to that tax era?

If we returned to that era, we would return to a time without a Department of Health – which means no health standards, food inspections, or oversight with regard to the water we drink, food we eat, or air we breath. There would be no standards for Doctors, or the practice of law, or any other government imposed standard we now take for granted.

In December 2013, President Barack Obama challenged his recognized opposition:

"If Republicans have concrete plans that will actually reduce inequality, build the middle class, provide more ladders of opportunity to the poor, let's hear them. I want to know what they are. If you don't think we should raise the minimum wage, let's hear your idea to increase people's earnings. If you don't think every child should have access to preschool, tell us what you'd do differently to give them a better shot. If you still don't like Obamacare ... even though it's built on market-based ideas of choice and competition in the private sector, then you should explain how, exactly, you'd cut costs, and cover more people, and make insurance more secure."

As annoying as that might be, it is perfectly reasonable for anyone to request, or even insist upon, specific methodologies and goals to be implemented when expressing an objective. But, if in this case, the Republican goal does not include inequity reduction, than they could simply state as much – which is, effectively, what is done when a request for specific solutions is dismissed, irregardless of what issue is stated as the goal.

The Tea Party Movement would like to see the *'Elimination of Excessive Taxes'*, it therefore falls upon anyone who identifies with the movement to provide a concrete blueprint designed for the achievement that goal.

As stated, clearly we must reduce, and ultimately eliminate, the National Debt. Once we achieve that goal, we also eliminate the principal and interest payments associated with that debt – monies which are included in the *'Excessive Taxes'*.

One way to eliminate the debt would be to transfer it to those who incurred it. We could use the government pensions of those elected officials who voted to incur the debt – rather than pay them a pension for life, we divert the funds to reducing the debt they authorized. If they authorized an expense for 'pork barrel' projects, than we also charge their district – make the district repay the pork and allow no 'adjustments' for other taxes paid.

Lacking evidence of any other means of reducing the debt, it is obvious that this suggestion represents what they had in mind.

In saying that was 'obvious', we can note that the 'Massive increases in the National Debt' – that debt which cannot be directly associated with World Wars, or clearly necessary spending – can be connected with President Ronald Reagan's doubling of the National Debt. This was then followed by the excessive growth under George H. W. Bush and the redoubling under George W. Bush, which is now continuing with the Obama administration. Thus, every past and current member of Congress – specifically those members of House of Representatives, which is the sole body Constitutionally liable for initiating financial matters – shall forfeit their pensions until such time as the National Debt is paid off. The tea Party would probably want to also attach the estates and inherited properties of deceased House of Representatives members.

Of course, if I'm wrong, various Tea Party Movement groups

can come forth with their own proposals. Naturally, any proposals would have to be as serious and Constitutionally consistent as the one provided here.

Responsibility for budgetary items rests with the House of Representatives, subject to Senate amendments which are approved by the House membership. The sole responsibility of the President is determine if the Executive Branch can comply with, or fulfil, the enforcement or administrative terms of the Law. The President then signs it – or, if there is an issue, Vetoes the legislation.

Congress can then override that Veto, and basically tell the President to find a way to administer it. At some point, the Judicial might then be requested to determine if all aspects of the Law are consistent with the Constitution – if not, all, or part, of the Law is declared Unconstitutional and is thrown out (invalidated).

Many Presidents have taken to issuing 'signing statements' – they might believe the Law to be unjust, or il-advised, or do not believe the Law to be valid and enforceable, and say so when they sign the legislation. A 'signing statements' might indicate the lack of sufficient votes to sustain a veto, or indicate that there is some overriding necessity for the Law, but that it goes against the moral or political grain of the President and his core constituency.

No matter what stage of the game an official enters into the process, if the House does not initiate it, a financial item cannot become a legal obligation of the United States – therefore no funds should be expended on it, and it neither adds to the deficit nor the National Debt.

To 'Eliminate Deficit Spending', we need to eliminate debt service on the National Debt, and bring about a balance budget. In an ideal world, that balanced budget would include funds for debt reduction, and then – having satisfied the National Debt obligations – allow sufficient surplus for foreseeable future obligations.

If we look back, we see that the House of Representatives has utilized Social Security Taxes to cover unrelated current obligations. They then went further and borrowed for operations which were il-advised, unnecessary, or blatantly wasteful. These were generally done as a politically expedience to ensure both their re-election and enhance their lifetime pensions, or assist them securing prominent private sector positions after they have been voted out or retire.

One might wonder why Congress appropriated foreign aid funds to cover items it has denied, or seeks to deny, the taxpayers whose money it is spending.

For example, why designate financial aid for the Palestinian Authority (PA)? Especially when the purpose is to assist the PA in paying off $4.2 billion in internal and external debt – why isn't that money going to payoff the American National Debt, or reduce its deficit?

Granted, in 2013 the amount was 'only' $426 million; and in 2014 it new amount was only raised $14 million to $440 million. But how much Obamacare would that have bought? How many new jobs might have been created if that money were applied to domestic needs, rather than to the debts of an organization a former PLO official acknowledged supported the Nazis during World War II, and still supports anti-Semitic acts.

Since money is fungible, it really doesn't matter what the PA states the funds will be used for. If those projects, such as the claimed building and development projects, were actually intended to go forward, that money is now freed-up for terrorist activities.

It was also stated that $70 million would go directly to the PA Finance Ministry – which has previously used its foreign-backed funds to reward terrorism.

In November 2013, it was revealed that the PA gave at least $50,000 as a grant to each terrorist released in "gestures" to the peace talks, and released terrorists are also given monthly salaries ranging from 10,000 shekels ($2,800) to 14,000 shekels ($4,000).

Thus, indirectly, we see a Conservative American Congress authorizing higher payments to terrorists than it does to those on Social Security.

The question is: "Where does the Tea Party Movement stand on the use of American Taxpayer money to fund terrorism ?"

We might also ask: Do Tea Party members even understand

when they claim peaceful use, they are only talking an accounting designation and not the actual use of funds? Is this how they intend to "eliminate?"

Of course we know that 'deficit spending' is simply another way to say we 'live beyond our means.' But, historically, that is what governments do. That is what the nobility of old did. It was the premise which allowed for Shakespeare's "The Merchant of Venice" to interact with the Venetian-Christian economy – a nobleman will squander money (politicians), then borrow from those they despises (Red Chinese), whine when the pound-of-flesh must be paid, then find a legal technicality to evade payment.

Members of the House of Representatives and Senate did manage to vote in an election year budget which would expire 30 September 2014 at a cost of $1.012 trillion. But we must remember that 144 Representatives, in October 2013, voted to default on the Nation's lawful debts – is the vote an election year ploy?

But, using the Shakespearean model, a sizable portion of our National Debt is held by Red China, and we routinely disparage the Marxist Communist spawn. Had those who voted NO prevailed in October, the legality of debt would have deprived China (and Japan) of its investment (combined, 15% of debt, with another 19% spread among other foreign nations). Basically the Republican NO vote was a vote to dispense with 34% of our debt associated with foreign creditor obligations – in total amounting to about $5.6 trillion.

The beauty of the legal technicality is that we would still have honored the 16% held by the Social Security Trust Funds and the 12% held by the Federal Reserve banks – voters certainly would not appreciate their elected officials creating a National Depression.

Since Social Security is a pay-as-you-go system, and the trust funds have actually been spent, current social security taxes would pay those who are retired – so that issue is one of: Would we have enough workers paying SSI taxes to support a system which keeps many elderly in poverty, and therefore requires supplementation? And that problem will continue irregardless the October nonsense.

As for the remaining funds, that too is money American owe

to themselves; therefore repayment is basically an accounting entry – albeit one that neither House of Congress would dare hesitate to order made.

Ostensibly, it is impossible to bring the National Debt to zero – because, in reality, roughly two-thirds of the debt is really money owed by Americans to themselves for future commitments they have made to ensure their own well-being. Is there any rational Congressman who would attack the "savings" of American voters?

Yet 162 combined members of the House and Senate did just that. In 2014, will the disorganized Tea Party Movement be among those who strive for their re-election, or will they be pointing to the threat those 162 represent to our collective retirement plans?

The American Federal Budget is a symbolic representation of the extent of American security. It represents American savings, which is why it is important to eliminate anything, and everyone, that threatens the long-term security of the average citizen.

Speaking of the first term of the recent Congress (3 Jan 2013 - 24 Dec 2013), Senator Bernie Sanders (D-Vermont) said:

"The Congress has just ended one of the worst and least productive sessions in the history of our country. At a time when the problems facing us are monumental, Congress is dysfunctional and more and more people (especially the young) are, understandably, giving up on the political process. The people are hurting. They look to Washington for help. Nothing is happening."

On the issue which caused the October shutdown, Sanders is on record as having asserted:

"The real issue here, if you look at the Koch Brothers' agenda, is: look at what many of the extreme right-wing people believe. Obamacare is just the tip of the iceberg. These people want to abolish the concept of the minimum wage, they want to privatize the Veteran's Administration, they want to privatize Social Security, end Medicare as we know it, massive cuts in Medicaid, wipe out the EPA, you don't have an Environmental Protection Agency anymore, Department of Energy gone, Department of Education gone. That is the agenda. And many people don't understand that the Koch Brothers have poured hundreds and hundreds of millions of dollars into the Tea Party and two other kinds of ancillary organizations to push this agenda."

Sanders assertion raises issues of the true motivation behind the attack on the Federal Securities, and the savings they represent – an attack lead by Senator Ted Cruz and, as the final vote showed, was fully supported by his Republican colleagues.

YES! The American Congress should "eliminate" all of the economic burdens imposed by the cost of operating the American Government. But how?

How are we to eliminate excessive taxes, the National Debt, and Deficit Spending? The three are interconnected – inseparable, in terms of anything presented by Senator Cruz or any other elected official who identifies with the Tea Party Movement.

Laws must be passed which strike waste and duplication from the Budget. The place to start would seem to be any law which pays out funds to the wealthy – anything which distorts normal, rational, decision making practices by providing an economic incentives which are not directly associated with normal entrepreneurial business formation. As is, we pay people to NOT produce a product – which means we pay them to keep the forces of supply and demand from working.

We pay people to locate in geographic regions which normal market and marketing methods indicate are ridiculous – when the payments stop, those firms often relocate to locations which are more rational and naturally profitable.

How do we control the Budget – bring receipts and expenses into balance – if the Congress cannot pass any Budget at all?

The 112th Congress had 42 debates, and failed votes, intended to deny fifty million Americans access to private health insurance policies. Finally, frustrated with their inability to deny access to private medical policies, we saw the government shutdown for 16 days – at an economic cost to the nation of over $24 Billion; which was more than the previous three year cost of the program.

What did the shutdown accomplish? How did it further Tea Party objectives? Was it even intended to succeed, or was it just a publicity tactic designed to agitate the American Voter prior to the onset of the Holiday Season?

It did make freshman Senator Ted Cruz a household name; it wasted a lot of money; messed with the holiday buying season, and, because it involved a vote to default on the nation's lawful debts, raised international concerns over the trustworthiness of the 'full faith' guarantee backing American treasury obligations.

Of course, had those who voted 'NO' on ending the shutdown prevailed, the government would have defaulted on its obligations and effectively eliminated the National Debt – and resulted in a new Great Depression. Poverty would rule the land, and all healthcare would be ... what? Free, or non-existent?

Once the National Debt was discredited, once the nation decided to go into default, there would be no current budget deficit – there would be neither interest nor principal to repay, but, as stated, two-thirds of that debt would have been reinstated. Albeit in a different form, or there would be no Medicare/Medicaid, no Federal Pensions, no Social Security, and nothing designated for future spending. But, with no real revenue to support them.

A third of those funds which dictate the long-term fixed cost of the Federal Budget items would have vanished – along with the American ability to incur further indebtedness to foreign lenders.

Obviously no elected official would condone any failure to honor the nation's obligation to Social Security recipients. To do so would instigate a new American Revolution – first streets, then in the voting booths, and finally, if necessary with armed rebellion; a rebellion which would see the military standing by their parents against the Congress.

If there were a real economic justification for the attack on broadening the private healthcare insurance market, then there are questions we could ask about other programs.

How many votes were held in an attempt to eliminate the tens of millions of dollars being paid Big Agriculture so that they would NOT plant crops, increase production, and lower the cost of the average grocery cart?

How many votes were held to remove special interest tax exemptions? How many Bills were introduced which would have leveled the taxation playing field, and lifted the excessive burden from those earning the least and balanced that by having those earning the most pay their fair share of the protections provided by the American system?

Has Congress introduced any Bills to eliminate off-shore tax shelters, or maybe require American companies to return profits to American shores and build domestic job opportunities?

How many attempts were there to increase the minimum wage, so that every working American could live above poverty level, and thus eliminate subsidy (often called welfare) that nation as a whole pays to underwrite the excessive profits derived by the numerous multi-billion dollar chain-store operations?

While there are many instances where it is, in the long-term, profitable for a government to underwrite various costs associated with the research and development of new technologies, there is no rational justification for underwriting the costs of established and profitable businesses.

We hear arguments about job creation. But the overriding reality is that no business will stay in an area where there is no profit. If the only profit is derived from a subsidy, then, as soon the subsidy ends, the business will leave. Of course, sometimes the business serves to attract those whose profits generate more than enough tax revenue to offset the subsidy – the subsidized industry serves as, what retail operations call, a 'loss leader'.

Unfortunately, all too often, Congress uses 'job creation' as an excuse to waste money and buy votes in various Congressional Districts. Ultimate, the money is squandered and programs that could return dividends are dismissed, or ignored.

Protect?

4. Protect Free Markets - America's free enterprise system allows businesses to thrive as they compete in the open marketplace and strive toward ever better services and products. Allowing free markets to prosper unfettered by government interference is what propelled this country to greatness with an enduring belief in the industriousness and innovations of the populace.

Imagine free markets unfettered by government interference.

Is that consistent with the constant distortions afforded to special interest groups?

As we saw in the previous chapter, both the protection, and the distortion of those markets are integrated deep into the Federal Budget.

Think about how complicated the tax code is. Hidden within it are a myriad of loopholes designed to ensure the wealthy pay less than their share, and thus shift the burden of their protection – the cost of military, police and courts – to the average employee.

The Internal Revenue Service defines a business expense in this way: "An ordinary expense is one that is common and accepted in your industry. A necessary expense is one that is helpful and appropriate for your trade or business. An expense does not have to be indispensable to be considered necessary." (Publication 535)

The problem emerges when the definition of 'necessary' is played with. Is a 'three martini lunch' really necessary? Several decades ago, there was a lot of agitation over those 'three martini lunch' types, but nothing changed.

The 'three martini lunch' was a catchy image which really had no defense, but then, nobody who really worked for a living would partake of such middle-of-the-day mind-numbing practices – except for stereotypical Madison Avenue types.

The fact is, there is no real means of determining what is a necessary helpful and appropriate business practice. Therefore, the standard is set by the industry participants, who are industries, or on levels within industries, where nothing is actually produced. The ultimate service industry, it produces only things which serve to benefit itself – the ultimate 'Special Interest Group.'

Until such time as the proletariat rebels, all laws are based upon preservation of the ruling class, who, on rare occasions, are also the ones who hold the wealth. As in the Shakespearean, their wealth is usually leveraged (borrowed against) to the point where they really don't own anything beyond the power they use to define ownership and interpret any related contracts.

When someone tells you they wish to "Protect Free Markets," you had better take a very close look at how they define those markets. In the *Merchant of Venice*, in keeping with the times, the ones who controlled the money were the Jewish merchants, those who controlled the "Free Markets" were the ones who borrowed and squandered the merchant's money.

Historically, those who owe the money will attack those who lend them the money. Unfortunately, whether the populous realizes it or not, the average worker is the source of the money the wealthy have borrowed. Therefore, whenever there is a possibility that the money will be returned (paid back), the wealthy label it "Socialist" and attack whatever return route has been suggested.

When the disparity between the worker and owner income becomes too great, the system begins to falter, and a new means of control must be established.

To control the masses, first count on their ignorance; then express goals without specifics; finally, the identity of the leadership must be as vague and undefined as the specifics of the agenda.

Generalities rule in a context where an enemy is named. In Shakespearean times, and before that, during the Inquisition, and subsequent to that, during the Holocaust, *The Jew* was the enemy. Even today, one need only follow the news and the same mentality is revealed – but, for now, it dominates Islamic politics, with some elements arising in outriding European nations, those nations that are on the verge of, or undergoing, economic instability.

At the end of 2013, Citigroup issued a projection which had the British Sterling becoming the global "safe haven" currency in Calendar year 2014. Since World War Two that was typically the province of the United States Dollar.

As with an "International Reserve" currency which is held by governments, or used to denominate the cost of their products on the international markets, a "safe haven" currency represents the target of foreign investment. Britain's strengthening economy

is the justification for it becoming the magnet for foreign investment. But, as noted earlier, in October, the "full faith and credit" of the United States was brought into question. As a result, the nation lost its foundation – global belief in its currency and debt based obligations.

Having achieved that, effect July 2014, airline user fees will cover 43% of Transportation Security Administration (TSA) costs, up from 30%, saving the government more than $12 billion over the next decade. Still, non-flyers will continue subsidizing security for air travelers; that raises an oft heard objection to Obamacare – why should one group of taxpayers subsidize non-taxpayers? In this instance the non-American travelers who fly on the same planes, and in terms of Obamacare, non-workers or those minimum wage workers holding one or two jobs in an effort to make ends meet.

As a class, airlines hate the fee increase, which they fear will hurt their business. Therefore one could assert that the fees do not protect the free market system; furthermore, it could be asserted that the airlines should determine their own levels of security; TSA should be done away with – in the same way other agencies should be dispensed with.

Of course, certain logical connections only work when we don't care whose ox is gored – so long as it isn't the one we depend upon.

We all know that air disasters and airborne terrorism can damage the general economy – something which affects everyone – and that brings airport security into the public domain. Still, user fees are reasonable, and therefore it is also reasonable to require passengers to cover the expense. However, that underscores the need for a risk/benefit analysis of TSA costs, which then creates political pressure to limit 'unnecessary' security procedures. But it then raises the question of what is really 'unnecessary' – is it only the protection against an attack form which has yet to be utilized?

Free markets demand that the market place handle the risks associated with the product – but that is not how it is played. The victims pay. They pay to clean polluted soil, water and air; they pay for a lack of, or improper, pre-marketing testing; they pay for the failure to ensure the health and well-being of their neighbor.

This brings us to the 'safety-net' wage subsidies provided to companies which paid the 2013 minimum wage of $7.25 and hour. The Tea Party Patriots Co-Founder Jenny Beth Martin has said that:

"Tea Party Patriots support free markets. In fact, it's one of our three core values. This means that we believe that employees and employers have the right to make agreements and enter into contracts without government interference, dictates, and mandates. History shows us that when the minimum wage is increased, unemployment rises.

Therefore, the advocates of the minimum wage increase are actually advocates of fewer jobs and less opportunity, and Tea Party Patriots will never support policies that kill jobs and opportunity for our fellow Americans."

But the jobs are lost because the firms cannot make a profit at that wage level, or find new efficiencies which reduce the needed labor. Thus, the argument is to either keep unprofitable firms operating, or oppose high productivity. Therefore the argument Tea Party Patriots put forward is for America to be less competitive in the global economy.

As of December 2013, The Congress decided to allow the extension of unemployment insurance to lapse, which, with the decrease in Food Stamp benefits, delivered a double whammy to 1.3 million unemployed Americans. But, since ending the benefits denies them funds needed for job searches, it ensures continued unemployment and increased levels of qualification for entitlement programs – which increases the cost to the government and overall harm to society. Actions consistent with the ultimate goal of the October Governmental Shutdown.

To that we can add the effects of sequester, which has kicked 57,000 kids off Head Start, and slashed nutrition programs for poor women and infants. Since 1964 – another infamous "War on," this one on poverty – the top 1% of Americans have more than doubled their share of the national income, analysis by Columbia University researchers indicated the "War" almost worked. Without it, nearly a third the population would be living in poverty – only have that number does now, and that number is the result of conscious political attacks on the poor, and intended to keep them destitute.

Pew Research established that income inequality is now at 1928, pre-Depression levels. At that time, the top 1% of families raked in 24% percent of pre-tax income, with 51% of pre-tax income divided among the bottom 90%. If this imbalance continues, we can expend another economic bubble and a new Depression Era, as we deplete natural resources and population continues to rise.

If the Tea Party opposes policies which kill jobs, how would they feel about policies which relocate jobs or deprive new workers of entry level positions?

In 2013, Colorado passed gun control laws which had the effect of dramatically limiting the sale of firearms accessories; as a result one of the largest gun manufacturers in the United States, Magpul Industries, decided to relocate its operations to Wyoming and Texas. Thus they are redistributing 200 jobs and taking about $85 million from Colorado's economy.

The legislation was passed as a response to the shooting at Sandy Hook Elementary School, and prohibits sale of magazines of 15 rounds or more rounds; in addition, it requires a background check on gun transfers. Of course, 'patriot' groups generally oppose any form of gun control, which creates a logical conflict. Do they oppose the gun control Colorado, try to retain the jobs, and thus oppose the creation of new manufacturing jobs in Wyoming, and the relocation of the corporate headquarters to Texas?

When taking narrow positions on issues, we tend to see the proponents ignore the secondary effects, benefits and hardships – the fact that every action has a consequence.

As it happens, Colorado might not miss that $85 million – a different piece of legislation also legalized the sale of Recreational Marijuana, with 1 January 2014 seeing the first of 300 marijuana businesses put to use their state and local licenses to operate legally.

That means the creation of far more jobs than were lost by the Magpul Industries. But it also means supply problems – where are they going to find a reliable source of cannabis?

There is also a secondary problem, one which will negatively impact taxation. Because of the federal government's continued ban on cannabis, these new businesses cannot legally obtain normal business banking services. Without the paper trail which banking provides, the ability of the IRS to audit these firms will be severely limited. Moreover, the legality of an audit might be brought into question under the Fifth Amendment – the absolute right to avoid self- incrimination in what could be construed to be, or involve an action, which can be interpreted as a Federal Crime.

Will Tea Party groups insist upon the right of the IRS to seek records that document interstate traffic – from a lawful grower in state allowing medical use, to a recreational use seller in Colorado. Does the Tea Party oppose free trade between lawful businesses in separate states? Or will Tea Party supporters fight to repeal any and all laws which could hinder these businesses from operating?

In theory, as was demonstrated with the prohibition of alcohol, legitimizing cannabis will have the effect of eliminating the criminal and black market elements of the business – in the same way bootleggers and speakeasies vanished after Prohibition's repeal. But there are politicians whose careers and finances profit from the criminal aspects and therefore will struggle to retain the illegal status for cannabis.

It should be noted that the move to criminalize marijuana began concurrent with the move to repeal Prohibition.

The replacement of criminal networks came into effect with The Marijuana Tax Act of 1937 – which became law on August 2, 1937, or slightly less than four years after repeal of the Eighteenth Constitutional Amendment on December 5, 1933. The effect was simply to re-task established smuggling networks to handle dry, rather than wet, product having a higher profit per unit weight.

Does the Tea Party Movement support free market criminal networks, with the inherent creation of corrupt officials, or will it strive to create lawful free market enterprises?

In either case, it must invoke government action to achieve its ends. The problem is, decades of research indicates cannabis is considerable less harmful than tobacco, and has positive medical uses or benefits. Thus, in terms of deficit reduction, it would seem rational to legalize and tax cannabis in the same way tobacco is legal and taxed.

Since I don't smoke – tobacco or cannabis – it matters little as to what their legal arability is. But, as a source of tax revenue, it is clear that it make sense to legalize cannabis. In terms of the cost to public health and productivity, it would also make sense to drop the production of tobacco – as we should know from experience, the criminalization of an addictive, or popular, substance is counter-productive.

The place to start would seem to be any law which pays the wealthy to distort normal, rational, decision making practices by providing an economic incentives which are not directly associated with normal market forces beyond the research and development stage of entrepreneurial expansion.

We pay people to NOT produce a product – which means we pay them to keep the forces of supply and demand from working.

We pay firms to locate in geographic regions which normal market, and marketing, methods indicate are ridiculous – areas from which those firms will rapidly move when the payments stop.

As we will see in a latter chapter, one aspect of the Tea Party Movement believes "bailout and stimulus plans are illegal." Thus these types of incentives would also be illegal.

When we suppress wage levels, then supplement them with entitlements, we are bailing out firms which we know are inherently unprofitable and inefficient. In a free market system, firms should be able to pay above poverty levels to all their employees. If they cannot, we must question their justification for existing.

Later in this book, I will offer a suggestion which would make it possible for some firms to retain low minimum wages, while also reducing or eliminating the governmental bureaucracy associated with the current network of redundant and overlapping entitlement programs. Ultimately, the effect would be to reduce government while enhancing the economic base of the nation at the foundation.

It is also illegal to interfere with the Market Place by paying firms to produce, or restrict production of their products – various agricultural products are being illegally encouraged or discouraged for the purpose of distorting the realities of free market economies.

Laws not only shape economies, but they also mold culture, so we must ask ourselves what sort of community would the Tea Party Movement create? What might we lose by not supporting it, what will we, as a nation, gain if we do?

Given that both action and inaction encourage the formation of both individual character and their subsequent behavior, what is it – exactly – that we wish our government to encourage? If we hold that America is a Christian nation, is it one that will emulate the Inquisition in Spain, or the burning and drowning of 'witches' in New England? What does it mean to uphold Judeo-Christian values, and how does the government fit into that scenario?

Healthy societies have governments which subtly tip things to favor a self-governing citizenship. In such societies, government facilitates the protection of nature, the arts, experiencing pleasure, and anything which allows individuals the pursuit of happiness, without infringing upon the happiness or beliefs of others. Which means not imposing your beliefs on others, or their bodies.

Abide By?

5. Abide by the Constitution of the United States - The U.S. Constitution is the supreme law of the land and must be adhered to without exception at all levels of government. This includes the Bill of Rights and other Amendments to the U.S. Constitution and their provisions designed to protect states' rights and individual liberties.

When America declared its independence, it also declared that there were *'unalienable rights'* – the rights to Life, Liberty and the pursuit of Happiness – which could not be infringed upon; it is the purpose of the Constitution to provide the framework which will protect those rights.

The first ten amendments to the Constitution constitute the 'Bill of Rights' and serves to define and facilitate basic elements which allow for an individual and collective 'pursuit of Happiness.'

All too often, we find groups who will assert concepts – like 'traditional values' – as the basis for infringing upon the rights of an individual, or class of people, to pursue that which will make them happy, in a way which does not factually infringe upon others, or their personal right to find happiness in what they deem to be their 'traditional values'.

If the Tea Party Movement is to abide by the Constitution it must honor individual rights rather than some vague and undefined set of values which are, in fact, imposed for the exclusive purpose of creating harm to others.

Consider the rough over the Affordable Care Act. The same law firm associated with the Hobby Lobby challenge to Obamacare's contraceptive mandate, is working with other for-profit businesses and some colleges and universities that are also opposing the birth control aspect of the law.

The long-term ramifications and cultural effect is interesting.

If you deny birth control, you also create situations where unplanned, unwanted, conception occurs; this creates an increased need for abortions. You then have the same individuals and groups screaming '*Right-to-Life*' for a fetus they effectively caused to exist. At the same time, the same groups do nothing to provide, or actively oppose, both pre-natal and post natal care. Then they also oppose continued medical care and education for those who would not exist if not for their intervention at the contraceptive level.

In terms of abiding by the Constitution, these groups are actively infringing upon the unalienable rights of the women who must raise those children who would otherwise have existed if not for the intervention by people who seek to impose their will upon strangers.

The 'Right-to-Life' groups, and other groups like themselves who focus on mandating other impositions or restrictions upon the private activities of strangers, will often assert '*traditional values*' as the basis for their dictatorial practices. The Tea Party Movement asserts an interest in 'Traditional Values.' But they shy away from defining those values as a single unifying tradition. Rather, they prefer to keep the definition vague, and speak of it in terms that change with their audience.

Traditions, hence 'traditional values,' are only philosophies which have been passed through generations. If they ever had a rational purpose it has often been lost, or forgotten, with time. It's the soliloquy from the "Fiddler on the Roof":

"You may ask, how did this tradition start? I'll tell you.

"I don't know.

"But it's a tradition.

"And because of our traditions, every one of us knows who he is, and what God expects him to do."

An all wise and knowing rational deity would impose laws that make sense – have a rational basis for existing. We know the Universe is imperfect, but it is a perfectly imperfect universe. It is out of balance and cannot can only pass through periods of balance – that imbalance is so all life could have choices.

We have the freewill, the choice, to impose our choices on others – it was done during the Inquisition, and by the Nazis. Each resulted in the death of innocents. If we go back in time, we see similar actions yielding the same results – a minority decides it knows the mind of a deity and imposes its will on another minority ; it achieves its goals by creating a 'demon', by demonizing a person or group, using vague and generally unsubstantiated assertions.

Strangely, it is a 'traditional value,' or methodology, which is highly valued by those whose common goal is to harm strangers.

The world is not imperfect because of demons. Demons are irrational – or the idea of their very existence is, and therefore does not comport well with a rational deity.

The world is imperfect because we possess the freedom to make choices and those choices interact in a random fashion. The purpose of culture, tradition and intellect is to get those choices to align in a way which will reduce the negative effects. But there are people who insist that their way is the right way, or only way, and try to force others to accept it. The very need to force it upon others proves it is wrong.

Statistical probability, chance, random occurrence, combined with causality is perfectly rational if freewill is to exist. Survival of the fittest is a concept associated with natural selection and evolution – but really applies to ideas and things which inevitably become lasting, rather than transient, traditions.

So, when we assert traditional values, we need to look for the rationality which gave birth to them. What made sense a 5000, or 1000, or 100 years-ago might not make sense in the current world.

In a world with geographic-positioning available on every cell phone, do we need the traditional teachings which once allowed pioneers to find their way in the wilderness? Do we need farming and animal husbandry, to shop at the local supermarket? Do we need to know weaving and garment making, so that we can buy a pair of jeans and flannel shirt at Walmart?

You wonder what these examples have to do with tradition?

In grade school and high school, I studies Industrial Arts. In college I furthered that study and learned to tech it. But, within three decades of my graduation, Industrial Arts was replaced by

Computer Science. An evolving tradition of craftsmanship which we all know predated Jesus – himself a carpenter, hence a student of Industrial Arts – changed. As our wisdom increases, as we gain what Biblical students would recognize as the 'spirit of G-D' – wisdom, knowledge, and understanding – changes, that which we term 'traditional values' must change, or we are denied the spirit.

Abiding by the Constitution is a means of retaining that spirit – of having happiness.

If we look to Obamacare, a program intended to aid people in their pursuit of happiness – by allowing them to be healthy – we find that all new insurance plans are denied the option of refusing coverage because of an existing condition. They must also provide a list of essential benefits which is to include basic vaccinations and cancer screenings, as well as free birth control – which is certainly less costly that having to pay for pre-natal and post-natal care every two years, for every covered woman of child baring age. But, that latter cost is what 'Right-to-Life' groups want to impose on each and every individual covered by private insurers.

We must note, as the Obama administration has, that the 1974 Employee Retirement Income Security Act, exempts church plans from regulation. Accordingly, a case which the Hobby Lobby attorneys brought on behalf of The Little Sisters of the Poor, which is part of a recognized, and exempt, religious organization could be classified as legally frivolous – it certainly has no meaningful basis. But the action moves forward because The Little Sisters of the Poor refuses to execute a form which states they are exempt. That is, they are refusing to render until Caesar that which is Caesar's, while hypocritically asserting they are obeying the one who set that rule for them to follow.

The reason for their refusal stems from the fact the form would allow non-believer employees the right to obtain coverage under the Affordable Care Act's birth control mandate.

Obviously, having taken vows of chastity, the nuns would not need the birth control, but they want to impose a by-product of their vows upon others. They wish to harm others with the assertion that to sign the form would amount to authorizing someone else to "sin on their behalf."

The Department of Justice holds that, "with the stroke of their own pen, [The Little Sisters of the Poor] secure for themselves the relief they seek from this Court. They need only self-certify that they are non-profit organizations that hold themselves out as religious and have religious objections to providing coverage for contraceptive services."

Their general counsel response is: "The idea that it's just a stroke of the pen trivializes the matter. You don't have to actually do it to be liable. If you are directing someone else to do the act that is immoral, you yourself are immoral."

Since the form allows employees to obtain coverage, the argument is that signing it has the effect of deputizing a third party to sin. Which is to say they seek to violated the Constitution and impose their beliefs on others – with those third parties carrying the full long-term adverse economic consequences.

Consider this, those adverse consequences are currently in excess of a quarter-million dollars and, over the next few decades, could exceed half-million dollars per woman per child. That's a lot of third party harm being inflicted in the name of avoiding sin.

Of course, society has a response. By not being qualified to execute the form, the Little Sisters' ministry effectively waves its exemption and declares it is not entitled to legal status as a religious organization – which then opens it to being subject to IRS penalties, and the legal consequences of a failure to file, or false filing, of tax returns.

But we all know that nobody really wants the laws of the nation to be adhered to, so they would find a loophole for the Little Sisters to crawl through. The result being that they uphold the right to hurt unidentified third parties by imposing ones traditions in a way which ensures harm and denies the pursuit of happiness – an unalienable right. It is nothing less than what would be done by al-Qaeda, the Nazis, or Spanish Inquisitors. But is it something the Tea Party Movement membership would support?

Promote?

6. Promote Civic Responsibility - Citizen involvement at the grassroots level allows the voice of the American people to be heard and directs the political behaviors of our representatives at both the local and national level so they, in turn, may be most effective in working to preserve the life, liberty and pursuit of happiness of this country's citizens.

As we saw in the chapter "Abide", the desire to deny coverage has the effect of imposing quantifiable harm on women, and in the case of The Little Sisters of the Poor, it is women who are imposing that harm on their own gender.

Under Obamacare, some 9 million women will gain coverage for maternity insurance; they will no longer be charged higher rates simply because of their gender; access to affordable health care will become available to some 19 million currently uninsured women.

As noted, there are those who would impose harm on these women. In a strange way, they would argue that it is their moral and 'Civic Responsibility' to inflict long term harm on women – but they will also argue they are not imposing harm. The problem with their denial is the lack of substance to refute the reality of the harm.

It is our 'Civic Responsibility' to ensure we do all we can " to preserve the life, liberty and pursuit of happiness of this country's citizens." If we deny them the ability to be healthy, or impose upon them tens of thousands of dollars in personal debt – on top of the national imposition which must also be addressed – we are failing that responsibility.

As we know, and can see in regular news reports, there are many who would return to the traditional values of Britain in 1843, when Charles Dickens published the classic "A Christmas Carol." They speak of 'Workfare' - which is a modern version of the workhouses spoken of by Scrooge. The words of Marley's ghost:

"'Business!' cried the Ghost,... 'Mankind was my business. The common welfare was my business; charity, mercy, forbearance, and benevolence, were, all, my business. The dealings of my trade were but a drop of water in the comprehensive ocean of my business!'"

Certainly these are not the business, or thoughts, of many in America today. But then, they were not the 'traditional values' of Scrooge's counting house, or the values which wrought the chains which Marley wore.

Do we hold as Scrooge:

""Are there no prisons?

"And the Union workhouses. Are they still in operation?

"Those who are badly off must go there.

"If they would rather die, they had better do it, and decrease the surplus population."

Obviously there are prisons, and many single parent families are the result of someone being incarcerated for an act – like the possession of a few marijuana joints – which in no way could be said to have caused harm to anyone. It was only after those who imposed Prohibition were rebuked that marijuana became illegal. As we know, many states are in the process of legalization, and it is only the federal prohibitionists who refuse permit this to be a legal business and new source of federal Tax revenues.

But, if you wish to harm others, you must do it through the assertion of false morality – known to be false because they permit cancer causing tobacco to be sold. Again, while denying smokers cancer screening and coverage; and now by attacking Obamacare which has moved to correct that very blatant immorality, or moral deficiency.

Of course we have the curious reality that marijuana serves to mitigate effects of drugs used in the treatment of tobacco caused cancers. Thus the legalization of a disease inducing substance can be accompanied by rendering illegal the very substance that would ease the suffering of tobacco victims – a double attack on innocent third parties.

As University of Kentucky Professor James P. Ziliak says,

"As of 1996, we expected single mothers to go to work. But if they're shelling out most of their weekly pay in the form of child care, they can't make sense of doing it."

Representative Paul D. Ryan of Wisconsin, views the poverty statistics more skeptically, and contends that the government has misspent its safety-net money. He and other conservatives feel there should be less focus on support and more on economic and job opportunities.

But, for the conservative view to be valid, those opportunities would need to pay wages above the poverty level, and provide child care programs for working parents – regardless of their incomes.

In an assessment of the fifty year long 'War on Poverty', Ron Haskins of the Brookings Institution stated:

"The nation should face up to two facts: poverty rates are too high, especially among children, and spending money on government means-tested programs is at best a partial solution."

The fact is, means-testing tends to be counterproductive. It does not address any the logistical problems associated with either unemployment or underemployment. In many instances it works to divert funds from the seeking of employment by forcing them to be used for mundane survival needs, thus making them unavailable when opportunities arise.

In the 1960's, poverty rates exceeded 26 percent, and may have been as high as a third of the nation. In 2013, if we count in-kind assistance such as food stamps, the rate is closer to 16 percent. But that ignores the fact that 40 percent of Black and 30 percent of Hispanic live in poverty; with 1.7 million households were living on cash income of less than $2 a person a day – levels equal to a third world nation. Moreover, in terms of birth control, 30 percent of single mothers live in poverty.

In 1959, 35 percent of older Americans lived in poverty, by 2012, in a large part due to Social Security, this was reduced to 9 percent, but, because of governmental mismanagement of benefits it is now increasing. The result of that increase is seen in the number of individuals delaying retirement, and filling jobs which would go to younger workers – this includes the elderly now taking minimum wage, or entry level work, which should go to the young.

But when do we still have that many living in poverty? Is it because we diverted Social Security taxes into programs which had no benefit to the nation? Is it because we were using those funds to subsidize the ongoing deficits, rather than creating an honest trust fund?

Depending upon the program, the average Social Security recipient receives between $500 and $750 a month. To live at the poverty level, a traditional husband and wife family – where the husband worked and the wife took care of the home – would need $15,510 a year (about $1300 per month) to be at poverty. Thus, a traditional "Leave It To Beaver," living a lifestyle which many assert reflects the 'traditional value' they support, is guaranteed retirement defined by poverty.

Once we guaranteed a retirement in poverty, we also created a situation where individuals would retain their lifestyle by working longer, or taking part-time work where the net wage is insufficient to generate taxes. The effect is to block upwardly mobile younger workers from entering the work force. Thus, the attack on Social Security benefits becomes an immediate attack on the tax revenues government needs to function.

That attack then becomes long-term. Before they even have the opportunity to begin their careers, young workers are displaced. That displacement deprives the young of income, and stability, which then delays the creation of families and that shifts the pay-as-you-go economics to create a further attack on Social Security for those who are now in their thirties and forties.

We can see the beginning of the long-term effects today.

Those effects appear as a scary reality: 3 percent of full-time workers live in poverty, as do a third of those not working. Yet we routinely here those who are working being attacked for needing assistance and not holding two or more jobs during a recession.

In the debates surrounding Obamacare, there is often heard the idea that one group of workers should not subsidize another. Is this argument valid, or just manifest selfishness?

Think about any standard price item – for example, milk.

The further you live from the farm, or the farm is from the pasteurization and bottling plant, the higher the cost of transport and delivery. Yet, we find a relatively uniform standardized pricing which does not accurately reflect the costs related to supplying the specific retail location. Basically, suburban and rural populations are subsidizing the urban dwellers.

Thus, to use the anti-Obamacare argument there should be no standardize product pricing. Granted, that is as simplistic as the vague and mindless objections the selfish generally use as an excuse for their lack of concern for their neighbors (their willful violation of the 'Golden Rule), but, in reality, it works and proves accurate.

Do we have a 'civic responsibility' to reduce poverty? If so, then we have a 'civic responsibility' to reduce as many unplanned for pregnancies as possible. But again, there are those among us who want the poverty rates to rise. They will not admit it; they will even actively deny they are intentionally attempting to harm others – but they know the consequences of the totality of their actions is to "manufacture" poverty.

In the words of Dickens, we might ask, does the Tea party Movement 'civic responsibility' mandate "by one consent to open their shut-up hearts freely, and to think of people below them as if they really were fellow-passengers to the grave, and not another race of creatures bound on other journeys."

Or is it a group which, "by one consent" closes its hearts to the true needs of others, preferring to think only in terms of its own acquisition of power and wealth?

The Tea Party Movement should be one which places civic responsibility – preserving life, liberty and pursuit of happiness for everyone – above petty politics. Government cannot compensate for the selfish among us – those who willfully promote practices which are, ultimately, designed to harm their neighbor.

Reduce?

7. Reduce the Overall Size of Government - A bloated bureaucracy creates wasteful spending that plagues our government. Reducing the overall size, scope and reach of government at both local and national levels will help to eliminate inefficiencies that result in deficit spending which adds to our country's debt.

Bloated bureaucracies justify their existence by being stupid. For example, in January 2014, the State of Maine faced $13 million in federal fines for 'overly generous' welfare system. The Federal definition of 'overly generous' is not discontinuing Temporary Assistance for Needy Families (TANF) payments to mothers who could not find work during the recession period between 2007 to 2010.

At issue is Maine's alleged failure to meet federal numeric requirements for TANF recipients to work while receiving benefits.

Governor Paul LePage stated: "Maine is overly generous in allowing a wide variety of exemptions from the work requirement, which are not recommended by the federal government, making it impossible to meet federal standards."

Granted, Maine does have "good cause" exemptions which include inclement weather, an illness, a lack of transportation and other reasons for recipients to avoid the work requirement. But it should be clear that these reasons are valid in any jurisdiction. It is also apparent that the Federal agents are pushing for changes, or reforms – via the proposed elimination of the 'good cause' provision – which could be harmful to women and children fleeing domestic violence. The result being an overall increase in the homelessness which has already started to plague the state.

As with other consequences, the federal agents will both push for the cause and deny the effect. Ultimately, their actions would damage the Maine economy and create a generation of children who would become a future burden to the national health and welfare.

TANF was created in 1996 as part of a major federal welfare reform effort designed to provide the type of temporary financial relief which Dickens' Scrooge attributed to workhouses and child labor. The TANF goal was to support children and their parents while the family works toward becoming self-supporting. But note, the period being attack is the exact same one which is identified by the national and international recession.

The Federal government wants to punish the State for not having jobs during what was arguably a Federally created recession.

The Federal law was designed to exclude exemptions from the work requirement, thus natural occurrences – such as the ice storms of 1998 and 2013, or the Polar Vortex of 2014, when trees took down power lines and half the state was without power – are not any more 'just cause' for people being unable to work.

The fact that the 2007 recession caused widespread general unemployment on a global scale, is not just cause for a failure to work. In fact, Republicans in Congress insist that if you haven't found a job after months of searching, it must be because you aren't trying hard enough – an argument they used to support their vote against extending unemployment benefits prior to their leaving for their 2013 year end holiday.

Denial of assistance – the people who, unlike the allegorical 'Good Samaritan', walk by the man who had been attacked, stabbed and robbed {Luke 10:30} – is the basis of their contention that an extra incentive (in the form of sheer desperation) is needed, so funds should be denied. After all, why should they support someone who is too lazy to overcome a recession, the illness of their child, or freezing weather and a lack of functional transportation?

Think about what this means for workers' bargaining power. When the economy is strong, workers are empowered. They can leave if they're unhappy with the way they're being treated and know that they can quickly find a new job if they are let go. When the economy is weak, however, workers have a very weak hand, and employers are in a position to work them harder, pay them less, or both.

Weak labor markets are a main reason workers are losing ground, and the excessive power of corporations and the wealthy is a main reason we aren't doing anything about jobs. But, as I will discuss in a moment, government is the cause of the weak markets.

Right now I would point to the perverse reality during that period, with its rules, Maine actually had a lower unemployment rate than the nation. Which meant that Maine's labor market was more stable than the national averages.

As shown by the comparison of unemployment rates, in 2006 Maine had a [December] rate equal to the national average, and at the end of the next four annual periods, Maine's rate was lower:

December 2006 4.6% vs US 4.6%;

December 2007 4.8% vs US 5%;

December 2008 6.9% vs US 7.3%;

December 2009 8.4% vs US 9.9%;

December 2010 8.0% vs US 9.3%;

Under the Federal TANF law, 90 percent of recipients are to work at least 30 hours per week — irregardless of the nature of the work available. In Maine, of 1,250 families, more than 700 – or 56% – include one parent who is somehow disabled. We thus have the victim in the street and the government not just walking by, but which pays its people to kick them and obstruct the Samaritan.

All states struggle with meeting the two-parent participation rate. Still, in Maine, the caseload has decreased from 15,000 cases in January 2011 to approximately 7,752 cases in December 2013.

Of course, the federal government believes that penalties inflicted because people were unemployed during a recession, or had a sick child, or spouse, will somehow increase employment in a state which has already shown it can perform better than the nation as a whole.

In factual economic terms, diverting millions of dollars from the state economy (the published figure is over $13 million) serves to disrupt natural business growth.

Normal economic multipliers dictate that for every dollar in circulation, seven to ten dollars of economic activity results. Thus, by removing $13 million from the Maine economy (via the taxes needed to cover that cost), the federal agency is effectively robbing the economy of $91 to $130 million in economic activity; that, in turn means it is robbing the federal government (through layers of lost taxes) of easily twice what is gained via the penalty.

The alleged punishment will actually result in a small, but meaningful, increase in the federal deficit. If we were to multiply this action by all similar actions across the nation, we would quickly see that a significant portion – if not all – of the national deficit is the result of "a bloated bureaucracy" creating wasteful spending – or denial of revenues. Moreover, Congressional incompetence is at the root of the problem.

Remember, all actions have consequences, and ignoring the economic multiplier creates a negative stimulation package. Thus we can find examples to support the idea that, while the Tea Party seeks to reduce government, the government seeks to reduce the economies of low population rural state to the point of destruction. In so doing, the federal government effectively becomes a suicide bomber – blowing up itself and the efficient state government.

Clearly the tea party is correct when it holds that Intrusive government must be stopped.

It might also bring to mind that a group of baboons is called a congress; a group of lions (classic symbol of many ancient rulers) are called a pride; fish join schools; and those who work together are a team.

So? Should our leadership go to school, exhibit pride in what they do, and be a team, or should they continue the role they seem to have taken, and be just another group of baboons?

I mentioned that government is the cause of weak markets.

Think back to the idea that we have a sincere obligation to "Promote Civic Responsibility." If we pay attention to economic consequences, this can be done while also reducing the overall size of government.

There is a an economic theory, it became popular in 1851 and has remained so to this day. It's referred to as the "lump of labor" theory, and I've already invoked it in previous chapters.

The basic premise holds that all labor market have a finite number of available positions. Thus, when one group enters the market, or remains beyond their normal retirement date, others will either be unable to gain employment or their hours will be cut.

If we think back to the 19th century labor market, we can see the logic. If we consider that logic in the context of population, we have two conflicting realities. In the first, a population has limited mobility and therefore the theory holds; in the other, you have high mobility, and the theory falls apart.

At the end of the 19th century, America truly became a nation of immigrants; those were exercising mobility in a way it had never before existed. Limited in the Old World – trapped in their defined niche – they crossed the sea and a new world of opportunities was immediately opened. In many ways, human culture entered a new phase, with new definition, and new 'traditional values' built on the foundation of the practical and transferable older traditions.

We often ignore a fundamental reality: 'Traditional Values' evolve. What we might hold to be tradition began at time and place which can sometimes be specifically identified, but more often can only be generally identified by era and cultural roots. Economic theories tend to have more specific origins, but still take on many of the characteristics associated with 'traditional values.'

Older people who remain on the job longer, are, within that industry and its geographic location, preventing their successor generation from entering the profession – unless demand for the identified skills of that profession are expanding within that specific geographic region, or growing population.

A geographic region can be defined as a town or community. It can also be defined as a nation or federation of nations – the European Economic Community, or European Union. When there is an aging community, nation, or culture, two forces come into play – the older workers fill jobs which should be available to the young, the young respond by relocating, and the community dies.

Boston College Center for Retirement Research economist April Yanyuan Wu, PhD, is challenging the use of "lump of labor" theory, by recognizing that America (and the world) has entered a period of high mobility I n which labor markets can no longer be defined as they were when Dickens wrote his *Christmas Carol*.

Wu points out that, given mobility and the availability of jobs in other regions, the decision by one individual to continue working does not impede a younger one from obtaining a position. In fact, the older individual might expand employment opportunities via the results of their work – a professor who secures a lucrative grant for their university can attract both students and colleagues to the institution. That, in turn, brings in more money for the community and opens additional teaching positions.

In terms of the average retiree, every dollar they receive that is above the amount needed for subsistence has an effect of creating jobs in the local community – the economic multiplier functions best when there is disposable income for home improvements, or the weekly visit to a local restaurant or movie. Deny the disposable income and you deny the jobs it creates through expenditures at local business establishments.

Most economists dispute that there are a fixed number of jobs available in any given economic structure, though they would not dispute that any given geographic location has limitations.

When women entered the workforce, there weren't fewer jobs for men, the economy simply expanded. The real issue was the mechanism which enabled that expansion occur. This is what is, or should be, talked about when the Tea Party advocates speak of the desire to reduce government and protect the free market. You can reduce government by providing the free market with funds at the basic consumer level – the level which lifts people out of poverty, the level of Social Security.

The Swiss have begun exploring the idea of providing their citizens a universal paycheck – all those who are not incarcerated, will receive a subsistence government paycheck, exclusive of any means testing. The mechanics of it can be worked through the tax system, and, while it would allow some the freedom not to work, it would not discourage work – in fact, it could actually promote the expansion of a more entrepreneurial workforce. However, Star Trek aside, it is an idea which would be impracticable in the current American culture.

If we look back at the way woman expanded the economic environment when they entered the workforce, we see that it should have been anticipated.

Women were already a part of the economic structure – they were being fed, clothed, sheltered – therefore the basic elements of their economic impact was already factored into the economy. That means, their subsistence needs already accounted for, whatever they earned amounted to disposable income.

Woman were now free to purchase items beyond their normal household budget; if they were married, their income augmented that of their spouse and raised the standard of living for both. It also served to make it possible to spend more funds on existing children, or to have an additional child.

All those factors, meant more demand for goods and services beyond subsistence levels. Additional children meant additional or expanded schools, which meant more teachers and support services which then carried the economic multipliers effect into construction and housing markets.

Which means, when we view the full economic spectrum, Wu is absolutely correct; but when specific locations are examined, the 1851 model proves to be 'dead-on.'

The issue is one of nation over community, and globalization over nation. If it is possible to reduce the mindless and detrimental bureaucratic intrusion into the economy, we could find the economy and tax base expanding naturally – with an associated reduction in Deficit and Debt.

Ultimately, Wu's reality only works in an environment which is both global and borderless. But pragmatically, it works when the local communities have no poverty, and mobility allows individuals to expand the economy where it demands expansion.

Believe?

8. Believe in the People - The American people, given their guaranteed freedoms, will thrive in a democratic, capitalist environment which allows individuals to strive toward ever greater achievements, innovations and the efficient production of needed and valued goods and services.

If we believe in the people, then we must also believe that they want to be the best they can possibly be. They are not going to take and do nothing – though what they do might not conform to the norm. Christians would recognize this in the words of Jesus to his apostles, when they asked how they would survive by preaching, he told them that the good [believers] would feed and shelter them.

If you aren't engaged in an activity which hurts your fellow human being, not only should they not hurt you, but they will also extend a helping hand.

As those who have actually read the stories know, the words "Everyone who asks receives; the one who seeks finds; and to the one who knocks, the door will be opened," were not just referring to some heavenly response, rather they reflected the response which was expected to a message of love and kindness being brought by the apostles.

Those words, and their message, was the concept which was reflected in the parable of the 'Good Samaritan.' Those who have read *Saint Paul's Joke* are aware that one of the key points is the fact that those who call themselves Christian often go out-of-their-way to violate the mandate of Paul, as authorised by Peter – who allegedly was the foundation of the 'Church' philosophy Jesus was bringing to the world.

In the "War on Poverty," alleged Christian leaders were so devoted to protecting their turf that they ignored the powerful tool that government represents in addressing the founding philosophy of their supposed faith – and that failure is being recognized.

Senators Marco Rubio and Mike Lee are on record as saying

that the American dream has become "unattainable" and that the nation's "first priority" should be reforms to the government benefits programs. Representative Paul D. Ryan concurs and has declared the safety net has "failed miserably."

"While we have programs in place that help deal with the pain of poverty, they don't deal with the structural problems,"

As noted in previous chapters, the traditional way of thinking no longer applies in an age when economies are no longer local, and may even be global, but, like any living organism, they still depend on their smallest cells for health. The smallest economic cell is the local economy and the level of poverty within it.

To carry the organic analogy a bit further, consider poverty to be the first signs of cancer. Cancerous cells no longer perform their designated functions, only their ability to reproduce remains, and it soon over powers the natural immune system. When it does, the abnormal cells spread and contaminate other cellular groups – until the body dies.

Curiously, there might actually be segments of the immune system which assist in the survival of cancer cells, in the same way they would assist any healthy cell – it's their function, but they are unaware of the true effect of their failure to discriminate between the cells which should survive to reproduce, and those which should be destroyed. At one level, the "Right-to-Life" advocates fall into this functional category – they promote the birth of children who are destined to poverty and crime.

They can be termed destined because there is no subsequent support network. As Rubio, Lee, Ryan and others have finally come to realize, we have people insisting children should be born, with no hands waiting to catch them, and practically no safety net to prevent their plunging to the floor.

Many cultures have, as a 'traditional value' the idea that, "If you save a life, you are thereafter responsible for it." The "Right-to-Life" groups are notorious for not wanting to accept responsibility for the life they save. To the contrary, prior to the Supreme Court decision which mandated that saving the life of the mother was justification abortion, these "Right-to-Life" groups actually declared they didn't care if the mother died – they were willing to see mother and fetus die, rather than allow the termination of a pregnancy which was going to kill the mother.

The "Right-to-Life"became, like the body's mechanism for protecting cells, an indiscriminate mechanism for promoting that which would ultimately kill its host. It knowing became a way to murder strangers. Or, as phrased by The Sisters of the Poor, it was a means of authorizing others to sin for them.

As we know, a similar problem exists with work requirement clauses in safety net laws. Individuals are told they need to find work I'm reminded of the old song, "Get A Job"

> *I hear the woman's mouth*
> *[I hear the government's mouth]*
> *Preaching and a-crying*
> *Tell me that I'm lying*
> *About a job*
> *That I never could find*

Given their guaranteed freedoms, there can be little doubt that the American people can thrive in the capitalist environment which they used as the basis of their democratic nation.

Rubio holds that the Obama "... thinking on this is stale and old and doesn't really address the magnitude of the problem," which it is and it doesn't. However, it is also hard for the public to believe that any Republican can correct the problems which they helped to create.

The Republican party has shown it is out-of-touch with the modern capitalist culture. They do not recognize that someone can be working hard without every leaving their home. They lack the basic understanding of 'Geek Culture' – the computer and internet age culture where someone surviving on pizza and pop in isolation can be the source of the next great app, the next Microsoft or Apple, or FaceBook, or Yahoo, or Google. These people are hurt by classic *"Preaching and a-crying"* that they should "get a job." We should not worry about the means they use to prosper in a capitalist nation

– we need to focus on those who inflict harm on strangers.

People should not need to justify their survival, in order to obtain a base level of life which can be defined as 'at' or 'above' the poverty mark. Unfortunately, there are enough evil people in our society to prevent that from ever being the American paradigm.

We can take comfort in the fact that they do not believe in people; they hold that everyone is like the New York City Police and Firefighters who fraudulently claimed 9/11 related Disabilities and cheated taxpayers of hundreds of millions of dollars which could have been used productively.

The problem is, the New York case wasn't about individuals attempting to do right, but becoming victims of circumstances. No! The New York case is, like the fraud which should be corrected, an organized effort involving a lawyer, a pension consultant, a union official representing detectives, and New York police officer. It was fraud by those charged with the prevention of fraud and criminal activity – the traditional realm of the criminal and the reason many do not trust their own government to protect them.

Instead, of looking to organized fraud, we have the issue of Maine TANF recipients whose State is punished because their child (or disabled spouse) was sick, the weather made it too dangerous for them to travel, or their car simply wouldn't start. As we have seen, the effect is to undermine the economy and, ultimately, cause the dominos to fall in a way which will bring down the nation.

One question is "Does the war on American poverty actually consist of endless attacks on the middle and working class?"

We might also ask if our programs are designed to increase the spread between the upper one percent and the actual working population? That seems to be the observable and provable effect.

Why do we seem to be actively blocking people from striving for a better life, while giving lip-service to helping them gain a solid footing with which to climb the economic ladder?

We have the reality that, because the rich have outsourced our key global industries, jobs are a real problem – and we penalize average people for not having the outsourced jobs.

As of this writing, Senator Lee has indicated he is considering legislation which would give states more control of Medicaid funds and elements of early childhood education such as the Head Start program. Ideally he will also move to improve existing anti-poverty programs by consolidating them into some form of an automatic qualification system.

Is there really a justification for individuals having to file for benefits through multiple agencies or programs, when the same 'proof' serves them all and the only real difference is that there are multiple intake workers creating an enormous administrative overhead.

Senator Rand Paul has allegedly promised to move for "relief from government policies and the opportunity to escape poverty," which represent a government largesse that saps the economy of its homegrown strength and serves only to instill dependence. More accurately, it serves to create individuals who are only skilled in navigating bureaucracies, rather that providing the type of capitalist backbone our nation will need to survive in a global arena.

Jared Bernstein, a senior fellow at the Center on Budget and Policy Priorities has pointed out that, "Cutting budgets and insisting on work requirements is antithetical to" a reality in which there are no jobs, and – through its manifest distrust in the capitalist system – the government is actively preventing Americans from utilizing the capitalist system to provide "a critical pathway out of poverty."

Once again, we must remember the modern paradigm is one in which the new, and previously unknown, has taken command of wealth creation. Could the "Leave It To Beaver" adults have seen, or understood, the ability of the average school child to hold in their hand a paperback book sized tablet that is more powerful than the IBM mainframe – and use it to talk to friends, or play 'Angry Birds'?

Think about it. In the 1950's, the idealized era of "Leave It To Beaver," that IBM mainframe occupied ten thousand square feet of heavily year round air conditioned space – and basically, all it could do is now done by little more than a spreadsheet app or part of a basic word processing package. Can we avoid 50's thinking?

Avoid?

9. Avoid the Pitfalls of Politics - American politics is burdened by big money from lobbyists and special interests with an undue influence on the peoples' representatives. The Tea Party movement is seen as a threat to the entrenched political parties and thus is the continual target of smear campaigns and misrepresentation of its ideals. We choose not to respond to these attacks except to strongly and explicitly disavow any and all hate speech, any and all violence as well as insinuations of violence, and any and all extreme and fringe elements that bring discredit to the Tea Party Movement. We are a peaceful movement and respect other's opinions and views even though they do not agree with our own. We stand by the Tea Party beliefs and goals and choose to focus our energies on ensuring that our government representatives do the same.

Here we have a problem. The Tea Party Movement holds that it is the target of smear campaigns, yet its supporters are routinely utilizing that tactic in their references to Obama – recall our friend SPARKY1845 on page 9. Not only is the smear, but we see outright malicious insult with not even the slightest hint of a redeeming justification or reference.

If the Tea Party Movement really seeks to become a valid aspect of the American Political system, its supporters must refrain from tactics reminiscent of the Nazi references to Jews, or those utilized by southern supporters of the KKK in descriptions of both Jews and Blacks.

When we read posts to various discussion boards and news sites, the Tea Party element is immediately identifiable – they are the ones who are insulting and whose comments lack any factual references in support of their negative opinions.

What have we seen represented in Congress?

Those associated or aligned with the Tea Party Movement have failed to make any affirmative statements or proposals which might serve to get the nation back on course. As a result, there is no basis for discussion or negotiation.

The destructive actions of October 2013, and the mindless attacks on the *Affordable Care Act*, seem to have placed President Barack Obama in a position where it is necessary to strengthen the executive branch and fully utilize its lawful executive prerogatives.

Naturally, the nay-sayers and slanderers respond with the type of charges which cannot possibly yield resolution, but have the effect of alienating the American public. One natural result of that alienation is the negative movement in approval ratings for both parties and the Obama administration.

Politically, it is always nice to have your opposition viewed negatively, but when it comes to achieving anything, those same ratings paralyze the legislative-governing process and propel those with executive power to expand their Constitutional mandate.

In December 2013, Rep. Justin Amash (R-Mich.) – one of the 144 Congressmen who, in October 2013, voted to cast America into Bankruptcy – told *The Daily Caller* – an online conservative news outlet – "I think it's scary the direction the government is going, regardless of whether you have a Republican President or a Democratic President. We have an executive branch that is getting way too powerful, and President Obama is setting the stage for something very dangerous in the future."

But, is it Obama or the SPARKY1845 types who are "setting the stage for something dangerous?"

Of course, a powerful executive does threaten the radical elements of society; it also provides them with extraordinary power, if they are able to gain control of both the Executive and Legislative branches and can therefore maximize it.

Congress has the responsibility to balance executive power, but it should never be driven to usurp it. But, either setting aside or gibing a nod to Republican Presidential history, Amash asserted, "I think as a Congress we need to step up and point out and take charge and point out when the President is going beyond his constitutional powers, which is frequent, and we have got to do something about it and we haven't done that as a Congress."

Amash voted to have the nation default on its lawful debts – debts the Congress created and voted into law, often as riders to necessary legislation – so we must ask where is this coming from?

Could it be these words reverberating through history:

"I don't recall te specifics of the speech, but I remember the broad themes, cascading out from the well of the Old Senate Chamber in a rising Shakespearean rhythm – the clockwork design of the Constitution and the Senate as the essence of that charter's promise; the dangerous encroachment, year after year, of the Executive Branch on the Senate's precious independence; the need for every senator to reread our founding documents, so that we might remain steadfast and faithful and true to the meaning of the Republic."

The words are a description of Senator Robert Byrd's oration – as heard and reported by Barack Obama on page 74 or his book, "The Audacity of Hope."

A few pages later Obama speaks to the way the "White House and its congressional allies disposed of opposing views; the sense that the rules of governing no longer applied, and that there was no fixed meanings or standards to which we could appeal. It was as if those in power had decided that habeas corpus and separation of powers were niceties that got in the way, that they complicated what was obvious or impeded what was right and could therefore be discarded, or at least bent to strong wills."

Think about those words; recognize them being repeated by those who would bend the nation to its ways and throw a childish fit – holding the nation for ransom – because they don't want the people to have medical care, or unemployed insurance, or care about the elderly struggling to live on Social Security checks which are significantly below poverty level income. They force people who have worked their whole lives, and were promised a retirement, to seek Food Stamps and assistance meeting their basic living costs.

They can rant about the transient poor, but their actions are designed to create a permanent underclass. If they were part of the

Judeo-Christian tradition, or actually believed in the basic morality of that tradition, they would rightfully be preparing for an eternity in a climate desperate for air conditioning.

The political pitfall which now confronts Tea Party members is one of nullification – the idea that states can nullify or void the programs created by the federal government. Historically, the idea of nullification has legitimate origins in the Virginia and Kentucky Resolutions of 1798–99 and was put forward by Thomas Jefferson and James Madison. But there is a pragmatic limit to the extent a modern society can tolerate a state having the blanket authority to nullify federal programs.

Were the Tea Party to politicize the process to a point where one faction can continue to create the type of situation the nation faced in October 2013, the nation will eventually falter and fall.

If that were to happen, groups like al-Qaeda cheer. America serves as a barrier to their expansion. It does not need to send troops around the world, in fact it is – as shown since 2001 – a boots on the ground strategy is actually detrimental to regional stability; buffer nations, albeit dictatorships like Iraq, become the training ground for terrorist legions.

In his memoir, "Duty: Memoirs of a Secretary at War," the former Pentagon chief Robert Gates states that President Obama does not accept ownership of the "War on Terror" and maintains the goal of "getting out" – of removing our troops from the unstable regions which are the target of terrorist incursion.

While the hawks might view that objective as a weakness, the reality is somewhat different. So long as American troops are in the region, they serve to distract local populations from the realities of the al-Qaeda aligned extremist groups. Moreover, they provide a reason why those regions are not advancing their standard of living.

As with the October conflict of the established funding for Obamacare, the Bush offensive was a no-win situation, which had no defined basis for victory. The eleventh hour effort to de-fund the Affordable Care Act was, for rational Americans, merely a last ditch effort by a child kicking and screaming across the floor in an effort to get its own way after being repeatedly told no.

The "War on Terror" was a slogan without a product. There is no reasonable manner in which terrorism, suicide, or mindless immoral criminal conduct can be universally brought to an end by the application of un-targeted force. We know the force lacked a target because President Bush declared that al-Qaeda leader and the architect of 9/11, Osama Bin Laden, was 'irrelevant.' That would be equivalent to Churchill or Roosevelt declaring that Adolph Hitler was somehow irrelevant to events in the European Theater during the Second World War.

When you declare war, you need someone on the opposition side who can negociate, and subsequently affirm, a resolution. You need to remove those who want war, and replace them with those who value peace.

If your goal is to balance a national budget, and avoid the creation of deficits, one of the first objectives is to remove the losses associated with military conflict.

Nations can only afford war at two points in their economic existence – when they have a surplus of resources, or when they have excessively high unemployment. Vast wealth allows them to absorb the monetary cost of war – though it might not allow for the political cost. And, when there is high unemployment, war puts the unemployed to work and provides new levels of employment for those who remain home.

When a nation enjoys peace and prosperity, unless it has an overriding need for resources and territorial expansion, it has no interest in military conflict – nor should it.

The days of the Cold War, when two ideological superpowers were able to face off and threaten global annihilation, are gone. In today's world, were a nation like Iran, or North Korea, to utilize a nuclear device, the only reasonable response would be their total annihilation. Convention military responses would be irrational. A modern economy does not need to waste resources on third world nations bent on self-destruction.

But if we remove war from the equation, all else is politics.

Maintain?

10. Maintain Local Independence - The strength and resilience of a grassroots movement is the ability of citizens at the local level to determine their own platforms, agendas and priorities free of an overriding central leadership. Exercising the clearly stated message of the Tea Party movement by its nature involves discourse about which policies and candidates best hold to our stated principles, and these various opinions should flourish and evolve at the local level.

We need to ask if the Tea Party Movement is an honest move toward government improvement, or a con?

Maintaining local independence is a laudable idea, but, as a nation, we live and compete in a global economy. Local platforms, agendas and priorities have no relevance in terms of security and individual freedom to relocate to other locales. By the same token, individual priorities and freedoms must take precedence over local political platforms and agendas.

Being independent, can a local community carry the burden of healthcare?

Can it afford schools to educate its young, or facilities to care for its aged?

Can local government safeguard citizens against the threat of a terrorist attack, or a more devastating and frequent form of life endangering attack – that of the elements and 'Mother Nature?'

Can local governments provide the food, energy or basics of daily life? There was a time when that might have been possible – but then we lived in caves, or made do with whatever shelter might have been available. That was a time when the population of the whole world was less than the current population of California.

Maintaining local independence is a laudable, but it has its practical and realistic limitations.

In the modern world, when we speak of 'local' we should be

speaking of our nation as a whole. Within that definition, our communities are our what we used to think of as the walls which defined our homes, and the fences which defined our property.

Yes! We do want to maintain the independence we enjoy within our homes; we want to set our rules of domesticity, and we want to instill in our children the proper way to behave within the home. But we also need to recognize that our homes are not cages.

There is a real world with which we interact on a daily basis.

Maintaining local independence is a laudable, but must also be realistic. Local economies and governments should be free to focus on serving the needs of the people, and not on the mundane task of keeping them alive.

Our elderly depend on Social Security and pensions. These are the foundation for old age – for a generation which lives well into the seventies and eighties, rather than die in mid-forties, as was the case when, in February 1890, Kaiser Wilhelm II introduced the Workers' Protection and Social Policy for German workers.

When we look at the local independence concept as a means of influencing the national agenda, the principle remains the same. That which makes it easier for local government to function serves the national agenda – without the right shoes, it is difficult, if not impossible, for the body to move across rough terrain.

Local governments are the feet of the nation, with the smaller communities being the toes which keep the body balanced. We have a Congress which seems to work overtime in its effort to cut those toes off. Today, people at the local level are concerned with their parents retirement and their own.

Birthrates are at record lows and small rural communities are feeling the effect are feeling the effect of the emerging negative population growth. The federal government needs to lift the boat by placing water under the hull – putting money in the pockets of the rural poor who will support local business and the national supply train.

Sadly, media outlets which should be praising the federal government for honoring local control – in January 2014 – took

President Obama to task for a patter settled 30 years ago by the Wyoming State Supreme Court and United States Court of Appeals.

In a 2009 tax case the State of Wyoming urged the courts not to drop due to the "implications of ruling on a boundary without the federal government and Eastern Shoshone being involved in the case." As a result, both the Environmental Protection Agency (EPA) and Department of the Interior were dragged into a matter.

The case involved the ownership of the land upon which the town of Riverton is located. The problem was emerged because the Governor of Wyoming, Matt Mead, decided to ignore the finding made by his own State Supreme Court during the rash of Indian Land Claims case which were prevalent during the 1970's and 80's.

In a 1980's water rights case, the State Supreme Court ruled that the Indians owned the land on which Riverton was situated. It is interesting that the State's finding had reversed a Congressional Land Act of 1905. It was taken as a stated fact before the United States Court of Appeals, Tenth Circuit, (in the matter of Dry Creek Lodge, INC v Arapahoe and Shoshone Tribes) that "the town of Riverton and other settlements are within [the tribal] boundaries."

In Yellowbear v. Wyoming, 2008 WY 4 (Wyo. Jan. 14, 2008) the Wyoming Supreme Court Rules 1905 Act Diminished Wind River Reservation as defined in a treaty of 1868. But this case did not involve the earlier parties, and set no legal precedent.

The EPA could therefore rely upon the 1980 case and uphold the clear statement of fact – "the town of Riverton [is] within [the tribal] boundaries."

Having lost its case, Wyoming Senators Mike Enzi and John Barrasso, and Representative Cynthi Lummis, demonstrated the same lack of character which caused the October Governmental Shutdown, and apparently (based on the 1980 case) falsely asserted "The EPA's decision has in effect overturned a law that has been governing land and relationships for more than 100 years. We are also very concerned about the political ramifications this decision could have for the tribes and the state of Wyoming."

Biased Media thus action distorted local court jurisdiction.

Fifteen Points

A google search produces The TeaParty.Org website which states it was created on: September 2nd, 2004, and asserts the Tea Party holds to these:

"*15 Non-negotiable Core Beliefs*"

1. Illegal aliens are here illegally.
2. Pro-domestic employment is indispensable.
3. A strong military is essential.
4. Special interests must be eliminated.
5. Gun ownership is sacred.
6. Government must be downsized.
7. The national budget must be balanced.
8. Deficit spending must end.
9. Bailout and stimulus plans are illegal.
10. Reducing personal income taxes is a must.
11. Reducing business income taxes is mandatory.
12. Political offices must be available to average citizens.
13. Intrusive government must be stopped.
14. English as our core language is required.
15. Traditional family values are encouraged.

Allegedly the Tea Party includes those who possess a strong belief in the foundational Judeo-Christian values embedded in the founding documents of American society, culture and government.

Unfortunately, the Judeo-Christian concept was not really a part of the nation's founding – though certain interpretations of the Bible were in such conflict that it made it necessary to assert there was to be a "Freedom of Religion" afforded all who were here. This is underscored by the site claiming this to be a Christian nation, a claim which undermines that basic freedom. It could be held that America is a religious nation, and a common deity governs all its religions. But that would grant non-Christians natural equality.

If we truly were interest in following Judeo-Christian beliefs, and held to the importance of an honest political system, then, as illustrated by the Wyoming case involving the town of Riverton, the media should be called to task for upholding evidenced deception in the statement from the Wyoming Congressional members.

It is nearly impossible to achieve the "*15 Non-negotiable Core Beliefs*," when members of Congress turn on their own State's Court and misrepresent a matter which has been settled law for over thirty years. Those individual should be removed from elective office – and, ideally, in November 2014, the people of Wyoming will take advantage of that opportunity.

It is impossible to '*maintain Local Independence*' when our elected officials willfully ignore the courts and belittle the federal agencies for recognizing those same finding – especially when the federal agencies were brought into the matter at the insistence of the State's Governor.

You do not downsize government by insisting that federal agencies be dragged into matters which they would have otherwise ignored. You certainly do not reduce deficits by insisting federal agencies become involved in matters which would have otherwise been dismissed – then rant disapprovingly about those agencies honoring what was apparently already settled law.

I would doubt that anyone would rationally refute any of the "*15 Non-negotiable Core Beliefs*." One might question the idea that owning a gun is 'sacred' and therefore on a par with the belief in a divinity. But it is a Constitutional right intended to allow citizens to protect their nation against any invader, or dictatorial usurper of power.

The uniform reduction of taxes, combined with the proper application of uniform rates applied to incomes above those levels necessary to maintain a reasonable basic lifestyle is necessary. The creation of tax codes which contain so many loopholes that only those who can afford skill accountants can access them – with the result that the wealthy pay less than the poor – must end.

Taxation should be simple, uniform, and begin at levels that are three or four times poverty level. There should be no need for complex tax forms, or tax accountants – much less for tax lawyers.

The Government MUST balance its budget, reduce deficits and, ideally, amass a surplus to cover any future military action, or natural disasters.

The government should not intrude on the lives of private citizens. This would, and must, not only include keeping them out of the bedroom, but also away from medical-economic decisions for which it assumes no ongoing responsibility.

There are life decisions which the government should not intrude upon. It is, for example, reasonable to allow a woman three months to decide if she wishes the responsibility of a child, but it is unreasonable to allow her to make an affirmative decision, and then saddle a man with the cost. If the decision is a woman's then the burden should be hers – not governments and not some guy who was excluded from the decision making process.

If the government wants to hold a man responsible for supporting a child – and exclude the woman from that cost – then the government must also grant full and unrestricted custody to the man so he can oversee and control that cost. Top do otherwise is to exert unfair, unjust, and inconsistent intrusion into the private lives of individuals.

If we are to support traditional family values, then we must clearly define what they are. If we hold them to be Judeo-Christian values, then we must define them in terms of the Judeo-Christian texts and teachings.

For example, Old Testament values allow a man two wives – to be treated equally – and assert that the primary inheritance goes to the first born son, not to either of the wives. If we go by the New Testament, there can be no divorce.

In the 2012 book, Saint Paul's Joke, we see the words and teachings of Paul hold that any who would have sex should be married – a statement written at a time when even the Emperor married a boy. Thus same-sex marriage must be held universally valid. Neither testament makes reference to same-sex relations between women, so absolutely no laws should exist which infringe on rights of women.

Of course there are those who hold their 'traditional values' to be different from those in the Judeo-Christian texts; since the Constitution forbids the establishment of religion, it follows that their systems – if clearly defined and established over several generations (as opposed to made-up as they go) – should also be condoned.

But it is highly unlikely that the bigoted members of society would allow the recognition of ancient value systems that are not their own; for them, 'traditional values,' or actions, are represented by the denial of 'traditional values.'

Consider the Judeo-Christian tradition and values which are the defining force behind the original practitioners of the religion defined by Moses, Jesus, Peter and/or Paul, and Mohammed. Each of these individuals are connected by the laws attributed to Moses.

Western cultural traditions and laws – as well as the laws of most countries – are tied to variations on the laws of Moses. Jesus told his followers to modify those laws, to update them in a way that would remain consistent with Leviticus 19:18 – "Love your neighbor like yourself."

The phrasing Jesus used, termed 'The Golden Rule', was built on the words Hillel used to describe all of Torah: "What is hateful to you, do not do to your neighbor." It is this concept which it the common 'traditional value' of America and the World – a reality which is part of the Davidic Prophecy of a Messiah.

To be valid and justifiably "*Non-negotiable Beliefs*," each of the 15 beliefs must conform to, and be consistent with, the idea that we will not to anything to another person which we would find hateful if done to us.

When it comes to illegal aliens, they are illegal because our laws have a system for establishing legality. But we must always ask why they came here, and if it is a reason we might leave the land of our birth to venture into a foreign land, where simplest interaction might necessitate mastering a foreign language. We need to then ask how we would want to be received.

In the Biblical verse, Deuteronomy 24:14, it decrees that, "You shall not abuse a needy and destitute laborer, whether a fellow countryman or a stranger." As Christians should know, Jesus was clear in mandating this of his followers. Thus the Tea Party has a 'traditional value' system which either clearly supports, or refutes, this teaching. While they might be in America illegally, they are most certainly strangers – thus the 'traditional value' obligation is clear.

We are also told, or warned, by Jesus that we will know people by their deeds, and should not judge them by their words.

What are the deeds of those who claim to be aligned with the Tea Party Movement? Do they abuse those who appear to be "needy and destitute" laborers – those who are on the lower rungs of the economic ladder, or have traveled great distances, crossed borders, for the right to labor in our fields?

Even *Core Beliefs* must have a foundation, a core doctrine or belief which is immovable and sacrosanct. That foundation, like the summary of Torah which Hillel delivered when challenged to do so while standing on one leg, and which Jesus then delivered as the *Golden Rule* is, in Hollywood, termed an '*Elevator Pitch*' – it is a single sentence which summarizes the whole.

What is the '*Elevator Pitch*' upon which the Tea Party builds its ideals and beliefs? Is it a variation on the *Golden Rule*, or is it the actions which seem to have typified the behavior of the old time, Reagan Era successor, Republicans – "*The Most Harm to the Most People, to provide the most wealth to the empowered few*?"

After the George Washington Bridge, Richard (RJ) Eskow wrote a Huffington Post commentary which opened:

> "Some Republicans are claiming Chris Christie isn't really one of them. Some pundits are claiming, even as scandal erupts around him, that he's a "different kind of Republican." He's more than that: He is the archetypal Republican, the incarnation of its arrogant, corporatist soul."

The archetypical Republican stereotypical image with which Chris Christie is being branded might well fit him. As we progress deeper into the critical 2014/2016 election cycles, we will learn if that image fits, and exactly how well tailored it is.

Eskow went on to characterize Republican hypocrisy:

"They claim to hate big government, but they want to expand the Defense Department. They say they want government out of our lives, then vote to control women's sex lives or manage a brain-dead woman's care from the nation's capital."

Ideally the Tea Party Movement has not be contaminated by this hypocritical behavior. But, it does hold that a strong military is mandatory, and there is some question as to the willingness of its elected officials to pay more attention to exerting power over the sex lives of woman, as opposed to the need to enact meaningful budgetary legislation.

'Traditional family values' are not built, or promoted, by strangers sticking their noses into our bedrooms. In most civilized cultures, such intrusions actually constitute criminal behavior. In biblical terms, it could be said it is a sin to expose someone else's nakedness. But, as most people know, there are those who get such a perverse enjoyment out of condemning sexual things, they will sit and watch for hours, just to ensure they haven't missed anything worthy of their denunciation.

We have the aforementioned attacks on same-sex marriage – it doesn't matter that St. Paul mandated marriage for those who would have sex, nor does it matter that the laws of Moses are only concerned with male bi-sexuality. Those who like to assert they are supporters of 'family values' will attack those who want to marry.

Fortunately, in United States v. Windsor, the United States Supreme Court determined that Americans in same-sex marriages are entitled to equal protection and equal treatment under the law. That ruling allows all Americans to engage in, and demonstrate, the 'traditional family values' descent people want to see upheld.

All descent people *love their neighbors as themselves* (Lev.

19:18), and so want their neighbors to enjoy the benefits of a stable relationship, recognized in law.

The attacks made on marriage by those who want to deny the loving couples entry into the institution has a long painful history. If you married outside your religion, without family consent, or to a member of another ethnic group, you were ostracized. It is not that long ago that it was a crime for a European to marry an Asian or African. Mobs could engage in lynchings with relative impunity – mobs composed of the same class of people who now proclaim they are 'defending marriage' by denying it to people in love.

The Israeli city of Tel Aviv erected a Holocaust monument in remembrance of the 15,000 homosexuals the Nazis slaughtered. Amsterdam, Berlin, San Francisco and Sydney also erected similar monuments – denouncements of similar Nazis atrocities. One can hypothesize that the difference between murder and 'the defense of marriage' is only in advocates the power to kill, but not their willingness to murder people for how, or where, they were born.

The Tea Party must oppose those who seem to take pride in putting "a stumbling block before the blind" (Lev. 19:14) and in many ways tainting the laws of our nation to ensure that we do not "have just balances and just weights" (Lev. 19:36).

Of course, they also stand with those who hold up The Book, but seem never to have read it, and certainly do not understand the random pages they've turned to. It is *Saint Paul's Joke* – those who criticize alleged violations while making it a point of pride to violate. They ignore the fact that Paul might have exempted new male converts from circumcision, but he mandated that all his converts – all who would follow Jesus – obey all the Hebrew Laws.

In fact, he went so far as to state that those who did not obey all the Law were not worthy to comment on even a Jew (one who was circumcised on the eighth day) who ignores all those laws.

It is a matter of referring to the written '*Traditional Values,*' rather than just throwing out the term and allowing it to resonate randomly through the population – where it serves to justify doing harm to others because doing harm is the value prized.

Members of the Tea Party Movement must always remember that even the Devil has '*Traditional Values*' which his followers hold dear and will honor at every opportunity. It is therefore imperative that one nonnegotiable mandate be the creation of explicit goals – demonstrative points that the process is on-course and has not been usurped by forces whose mandate is to destroy.

One area of specificity is that of business ethics, and, because politics involves the handling of the nations finances – its profits in terms of emotional and tangible assets – the political ethics.

In the Jewish texts it is taught of business, thus of politics:
"Were you honest in your business dealings? This is the first question because it's the true measure of one's success in life. There is no greater temptation to cheat than is a business setting where one can earn more profits.

If you can overcome this great temptation, you will reach a high level of character that others esteem. Your customers, employees and those you do business with want to patronize your business. When you are honest, your business grows. You also have the right answer in the heavenly court. As the Medrash says, 'If one is honest in his business dealings and people esteem him, it is accounted to him as though he had fulfilled the whole Torah'" (Babylonian Talmud, Shabbat 31a; Mekhilta B'Shalach 1)

One value that politicians ignore seems to be the one in "Our work is meaningless unless it is to do good" (Ecclesiastes 3:12–13).

We do not need to invoke scripture to be able to respect that which defines 'traditional values', but we should acknowledge the reality that its laws emerged – evolved – from practices which were proved to make sense and work over time.

Some assert divine origins for the knowledge and laws. That is not an issue; in fact it is a universal commonality – as are various variations on the 'Golden Rule.'

There is no need for a religious justification, or reference, simple logic reveals the wisdom behind the idea that, when meeting someone new, you both demonstrate and echo proper manners.

Educational Values

We know that the deficit is a problem. There is no question that the national debit is a horrific burden we are heaping upon our children, grandchildren and even great-grandchildren. And there is no rational economist, or accountant, who would argue that we do not need a balanced budget.

There was a time when economists didn't care about debt.

In those bygone days, the population was growing and it was believed that each generation would be wealthier than the last.

But, more important than growing wealth was the belief that inflation would solve the known fixed long-term debt problem. We therefore heard them tell Congress, "Debt is not a problem."

Naturally, in the mind of those testifying, it wasn't a problem – whatever debit was incurred could be monetized. They didn't even have to worry about being taken to task if they were wrong – before anyone realized that were, they'd have gotten their wealth, enjoyed it, and died. The testimony associated with their names to be forgotten, or not even known to those burdened by reality.

Monetize the nation's debt, the Federal Reserve purchases our own treasury debt which has the effect of increasing the nation's money supply. It is a form of shell game which converts debt into money (hence monetization).

Since the Federal Reserve prints the money, and secures it with treasury debt, the effect is akin to you saving for retirement by placing IOU's in a piggy back and pocketing the money. So long as you have a good credit rating, other people will buy your IOU's and you can pay yourself back, or buy something tangible which will hold, or increase its intrinsic real value (e.g., Gold, or Silver).

Since money is, effectively, a government IOU, the Federal Reserve is using one IOU to buy another. Constitutionally, the American Dollar should be denominated in terms of gold and silver, with the states required. In fact, Article 1 Section 10 mandates that "No State shall ...; make any thing but gold and silver Coin a Tender in Payment of Debts; ..."

Obviously, the moving of gold and silver coin would be far more cumbersome than moving paper money which is effectively a gold and silver depository receipt. That was actually the origin of paper money. Some seven hundred years ago, China would require foreign merchants to deposit their gold and silver at the border, in exchange for paper currency which they could use to conduct their transactions within China's borders.

Former Congressman Ron Paul of Texas has apparently said the Federal Reserve is unconstitutional because it no longer deals in 'real currency.' In many ways he is correct.

On August 15, 1971 President Richard Nixon effectively took us off the gold standard by ending the international convertibility of dollars to gold. Prior to that time, an individual could obtain an ounce of gold in exchange for $35; prior to 1932, the cost would have been slightly under $21 – a dollar is actually a unit of measure equal to one-twentieth of an ounce of gold. Prior to 1918, you could obtain gold for less than $19 an ounce – or about dollar less than its defined value.

The critical issue involved is somewhat legalistic. Only the states are mandated to accept gold and silver coin – a requirement which does not extend to citizens. Constitutionally, the Federal government is the only agency which can produce, or coin, money; because of that, whatever the Federal government declares to be currency is currency.

With the dollar pegged to gold, and the exchange rate fixed, it was worthwhile for other nations to fix their currency against the dollar. All of the currencies gained a standard, or fixed exchange rate. But if currency values float against gold, you have a new game.

Thought of in another way, every time the number of dollars needed to purchase a troy ounce of gold increased, the dollar was devalued. When you devalue the currency used to denominate fixed debt, you effectively pay back the debt at a discount.

In terms of troy ounces of gold, if in 1970 you borrowed $105 and purchased three ounces of gold, then, in January 2014, paid back the debt (spot price of gold $1247) – you would still have roughly 2.916 troy ounces in your pocket.

When, eventually, the government is actually called upon to repay its debts – assuming that it has not continued to amass them through deficit spending – they have monetize the nation's debt in a way that means they never really had to pay it back. That is why, under Nixon, it was assumed the debt was meaningless.

Unfortunately, Ronald Reagan doubled the national debt, and then George H.W. Bush increased it further – under Clinton it was stable, with a slight budgetary surplus – then George W. Bush both doubled the debt, and caused a recession which was server enough to made it impossible to balance, or stabilize, the budget.

That is precisely the type of irresponsible behavior which the Tea Party opposes. As all available budgetary figures reveal, the Obama administration managed to slow the rate of deficit growth, but not sufficiently to prevent the continued rapid growth in debt.

If the Tea Party Movement is successful, and honors its own mandate, it will find a way to expand upon the work begun by Obama and bring the budget into a position where the debt will be properly monetized to the benefit of subsequent generations.

The problem is the October 2013 Governmental Shutdown experience. Recall the words of Jesus – not by their words, but by their deeds shall you know them. The Shutdown threatened the nation with default on its lawful debts. That would have eliminated the debt – bankruptcy does that – but it would also have plunged the global economy into a Depression from which China and other Asian nations, along with the oil rich nations of Islam, would have emerged as the global economic superpowers.

It is a matter of education, and comfort with numbers.

In that regard, the American work force has some of weakest mathematical and problem-solving skills in the developed world.

The Organization for Economic Cooperation & Development, conducted a survey which revealed that adults in the United States score far below average – of twelve developed nations tested, only Italy and Spain scored lower. Considering that neither of those nations has been considered a 'power' for well over six centuries, that isn't much of an accomplishment.

Countries in Europe and Asia already have schools which are superior to American schools are now gaining in the area of worker training, and steadily improving both their educational systems and that training.

Can the United States justify a continued pattern ignoring the lessons from those high-performing countries? Can it ignore the reality of policies designed to outsource both jobs and domestic wealth? Are average Americans really willing to allow the special interests to surrender their competitive position in the world? Are those who are aligned with the Tea Party Movement willing to allow special interests to plunge the nation into bankruptcy?

Remember the fourth point of the '*15 non-negotiable core beliefs*': "Special interests must be eliminated." Is that real, or is it just a statement intended to con the gullible into financing their own destruction?

Consider this, the traditionally socialist Scandinavian nation of Finland has for years been in the highest global ranks in literacy and mathematical skills.

One reason dates back to the postwar period, when Finns first began to consider creating comprehensive schools that would provide a quality, high-level education for poor and wealthy alike. These schools stand out in several ways, without the complications and costs of means testing, they provide daily hot meals; health and dental services; psychological counseling; and an array of services for families and children in need.

When we think about those who question providing these services to American children, we must look at the term 'in need', not in the sense of third world poverty, but in the way that it would apply in the Good Samaritan parable. You look at the situation, and respond to that – you do not first check their credit history or see what is left in their wallet.

In Finland, all high school students must take one of the most rigorous required curriculums in the world, including physics, chemistry, biology, philosophy, music and two foreign languages.

If this were done in America, there would be outrage – the idea of an educated populous contradicts the core Creationist beliefs, as well as those who are in denial about the effect humanity is having on the climate and planet as a whole. Which, when it comes from those who profess a biblical belief, is somewhat funny – the core commandment to Adam was to be a guardian to the earth, so even the possibility that there is a human factor involved should get them working to ensure there isn't and never will be.

Again, see alleged traditional values and core beliefs emerge which, rather than discourage harm, seem to encourage it. Is this the soul of the Tea Party Movement, or does it strive to improve the human condition for all Americans?

By professionalizing the teacher corps and raising its value in society, Finland has made teaching the country's most popular occupation – what do Americans study? We know that more than 30 percent of American adults hold bachelor's degrees, with women becoming the majority of degree holders. We also know Asian-Americans are the nation's best-educated racial group, with 50.3% hold bachelor's degrees, 19.5% hold graduate degrees, and the field of Education is not at the top of their list.

But we also know that, with a declining population and an older age for birth of the first child, teaching is not a growth career – especially in a nation which pays a football coach a higher salary. We must wonder why, in a nation whose founding fathers also founded some of the worlds best colleges and universities, their descendants education is to pound each other on a sports field.

Finland offers programs which recruit from the top quarter of the graduating high school class, while the United States is a land where a recent report by the National Council on Teacher Quality called teacher preparation programs "an industry of mediocrity." Certainly it should be a national objective to determine the area of speciality which is best suited for the American character, and then to target the production of teachers and students to achieve that objective.

Is the Tea Party Movement involved with any grassroots goal

associated with fulfilling a recognized need for specific long-term skills? Does its membership even concern itself with the need for such skills? Where will we find the people whose knowledge base allows for long-term deficit reduction and the creation of a stable budgetary process. Certainly this cannot come from individuals trained in litigation and short-term adversarial confrontation.

Regardless of the level of population decline, America would benefit from the Finish model of requiring its junior high and high school teachers to have stronger academic credentials, and they are rewarded with higher salaries.

In Canada we find a nation which strives to eliminate or at least minimize the funding inequality that would otherwise exist between poor and wealthy districts. America – thanks to *No Child Left Behind* – rewards the wealthiest, highest-spending districts, which receive and spend about twice as much per pupil as the lowest-spending districts.

In order to ensure the funding disparity, the testing structure established as the funding criteria for *No Child Left Behind* was designed specifically to evaluate different population groups. The law tests successive classes rather than the changes achieved over progressive years with the same student group. Thus small schools are punished for having intelligent children in one class and average ones in its successor class. It also seems to guard against a reversal of that pattern.

In some states, like California, spending ratios between rich and poor districts are more than three to one. Having noted Asian-American performance, it is worth also noting that Shanghai has taken several approaches to repairing the disparity between strong schools and weak, as measured by infrastructure and educational quality. Poor schools might be closed, reorganized, or merged with higher-level schools; rural schools are provided the funds necessary to construct new buildings or update old ones – with incentives for more qualified teachers to relocate to rural districts.

If America does not improve its attitude toward both primary education, and early childhood development, it will rapidly become a Third World power – a level which will also be attained when it has fully depleted its "clean energy" fossil fuel reserves and becomes dependent upon its massive coal deposits.

Without clean liquid fuel, or electrical power cells which will allow vehicles to travel at highway speeds for a minimum of sixteen hours a day (with less than a five hour charging period), America's military will be confined to domestic operations – no longer will wars be fought on foreign soil – the nation will be able to launch a single devastating attack, without the ability to invade and occupy; war will be reduced to long distance drone induced genocide.

In an address to the nation, President Obama stated that:

"Our success as a country depends on more than the success of our broader economy – it depends on the success of the American people. It depends on your ability to make ends meet, provide for your families, and, with a little hard work, feel like you can get ahead."

If America continues to export its industries and technologies – with a commensurate weakening of its educational structure and undermining of its foundational economy – failure is more assured than any continued success.

The prospect of assured failure is the motivation driving the grassroots elements of the Tea Party Movement to insist that the 'old way' of doing things – the way which has dominated politics since the 'red scare' McCarthy Era, be brought to an end. People have opened their eyes and seen that the McCarthyist buzzwords – the mindless screaming of 'socialist' whenever a Christian seeks to adhere to the explicit teachings of Jesus – are self-destructive.

Antichrists and anti-Semitics take pride in their use of the 'socialist' term. They ignore the reality that our nation is borrowing from 'Socialist' nations, just to survive, while making the rich richer.

We have seen how monetization of the nation's debt can be used to defraud its creditors of actual wealth. This is achieved by taking advantage of their lack of financial education. In business schools students take courses in taxation, often described as "how to keep your il-gotten gains out of the hands of the tax collector."

They are also taught to use bankruptcy laws as a tool for amassing wealth – use of leverage (borrowing) to acquire income producing businesses with little or no real investment, allows the buyer to bleed the investment dry. The use of corporate structures, or shells, allow owner assets to be shielded from creditor claims – in some cases, expenses deducted against income are paid to other corporations owned by the same individuals.

Once bleed of all profits, with a value that no longer reflects the original purchase price, the debt service (payment of mortgage), is pocketed and the property goes into foreclosure or bankruptcy – with the derived funds securely in the investors pocket.

The same business classes teach that to build an economy, you begin with ensuring that the workers have the funds to spend to promote the process – the economic multiplier effect.

When Finland abandons means testing and provides meals to all its students, it achieves two things: it ensures the children have reliable and health diets, and it frees money for the parents to spend in local stores. The latter creates or sustains local jobs, and that then creates the need for supplier support networks. Paying good salaries to teachers, who would also be local residents, adds more capital to the local economy and more demand for goods and services.

If we repeat this with retirees, and those holding minimum wage positions, we can easily envision the means by which the local economies can experience a natural, organic growth. That process does not automatically follow the artificial incursion of a dominant industry whose existence has no natural justification for being in a specific geographic location.

The current Entitlements system has serious flaws. One is that of duplicated means testing – by one analysis, often involving 76 duplicated filings of the same documentation. Curiously, it would be cheaper to issue a monthly check to every citizen, with the requirement that they file an annual tax form which reports that payment and all other income.

Possibly, assuming the checks equaled poverty level income,

a personal deduction equal to that amount would render it tax free, and an additional deduction of the same amount would encourage working. Social Security would also be reported and deemed free of taxation, with all other income – regardless of source – taxed at a flat rate.

This would eliminate the Entitlement bureaucracy, which is an easy means of reducing the size and cost of government. Since you know who is getting the check, that Social Security Number could be matched to filed tax returns and cross referenced against employer or corporate filings.

The checks payment system could be initiated with the filing of a birth certificate and corresponding Social Security Number a month prior to the citizen's 18th birthday, or the first birthday after an adult becomes a naturalized citizen – in which case it would be accompanied by the Social Security and Naturalization papers.

In the case of incarcerated individuals, the checks would go to the state penal system where they are held. Where relevant, any Social Security benefits would also go to the penal system.

If the Tea Party Movement really wishes to reduce the cost of government, it will need to devise some system – like the income based one described here – which will eliminate, not complicate the system for alleviating poverty while also boosting the fundamental economic foundation of the nation that is our communities.

The idea that some will not work is not a problem. Those who are inclined to avoid honest work will do so, whether they are *at work* or not. America does not need inefficient or obstructionist workers reducing corporate productivity; at the same time, it will benefit from those creative individuals whose creativity requires a development period before the rewards for the nation as a whole becomes apparent.

The creation of a *shadow economy* involving illegal aliens or criminal activities could become more difficult, and a failure to file a tax return, or filing a false return, might provide law enforcement with basic level of criminal conviction. Claiming a monthly check would also expose a suspected criminal's location.

Congress

In July 2013, House Speaker John Boehner (R-Ohio) stated, "[Congress] ought to be judged on how many laws we repeal. We've got more laws than the administration could ever enforce."

In January 2014, with an Unemployment Benefits Extension renewal pending, the GOP-led House passed legislation which would require that any breach of security in an Obamacare website to be made public within two days.

In terms of limited government, the Nation has too many laws, and far too many which duplicate, or complicate other laws. To many agencies are dealing with the collecting of identical data before they can assist America's citizens, or direct them to necessary resources – be they informative, or licensing.

As Boehner asserted in an interview with CBS News' Bob Schieffer, "[Congress] should not be judged on how many new laws [they] create." They should be clarifying laws and addressing issues which benefit the people they are paid to serve, but in reality, they seem to be paid to take time off.

In 2013, the House scheduled 239 days off; they increased that number for 2014. Could you imagine any business which had its management vanish for 239 out of every 365 days – receiving about $1,400 for each day 'worked'. Those they are paid to serve are expected to put in 250 business days a year ibn order to earn the money, to pay the taxes, which pay the salaries of Congress.

Of the days in a year, 104 constitute weekends and 10 days are legal bank holidays; if we exclude overtime days, exclusive of their two week vacation, the average worker receives 114 societally designated days off. Even if we allow for twenty-five paid holiday and sick days, Congress still takes one hundred days more than those they work for. That's over three full months when they are neglecting the nation's business; yet they expect a generous lifetime pension.

The Tea Party asserts it stands for limited government, free markets, and traditional values.

Is it a traditional value to grant workers more free time than their employers, and also grant them larger retirement benefits – at the end of a few years of neglecting their duties and responsibilities?

The 2014 House calendar revealed members of Congress will only work only 113 days; in 2012 they only worked 107 days – which renders the Republican controlled Congress the least productive in modern history.

Given their past track record, how much less productive, how much more time can they spend avoiding the people's business, can we expect them to be after the 2014 election, when all 435 seats in the United States House of Representatives will be in play?

We know how the old term ended, and the new term began.

At the end of 2013, unemployment benefits for 1.3 million workers were allowed to expire; Congress went home to enjoy their New Year's Parties while those families wonder how they would pay the heating costs associated with the Polar Vortex which swept the nation.

Upon their return, the plight of the unemployed, who were still awaiting the jobs lost in the Bush 2007 Recession to either be restored or replaced, were again ignored. The first order of business for the House of Representatives was to focus on Affordable Care Act Cyber Security. The republicans decided that it was necessary to pass legislation which would require the secretary of Health and Human Services to tell people of any security breach which might compromise their private data – something already incorporated into the law, and therefore an unnecessary redundancy whose only purpose is to waste legislative time.

Interestingly, there haven't been any successful breaches of the system, nor is there information that isn't freely obtainable via a standard Google search. The site does require the inputting of names, birth dates, email addresses and social security numbers, but the government site is a far less attractive than that of TARGET and NIEMAN MARCUS, both of which were hacked, and yielded, or compromised the credit card data for some 110 million people over the holiday buying period.

More importantly, the Congress knew of there were ACA site glitches in October, and, with regard to offering any directives for reporting of repairing, totally ignored them – choosing rather to shut the government in an effort to block funded efforts to expand medical care to the working poor, and those have been denied because of prior medical conditions.

It is a matter of priorities and service to the nation. Members of Congress have demonstrated they would rather duplicate prior legislation than prevent their constituents from freezing – or being able to get medical care for problems brought about by abnormal weather patterns.

If the Tea party is to justify its mandate, it needs to remove these irresponsible incompetents from office. The opportunity to do so comes in November 2014.

Will the American people elect another goof-off Congress to serve their needs until 2016, or will Americans seek people who are actually willing to do their jobs?

Have members of the Tea Party demonstrated a willingness to work, to actually address the problems facing America over the course of the next decade? If so, than, if elected into the role of a House majority, wouldn't they be able to put forth an honest and competent individual to serve as President? Could they locate an individual who is conducive to the programs which define the Tea Party agenda?

The Tea Party asserts their goal is fiscal responsibility, thus we can assume the rest of the Republican Party must shoulder the blame for the failure of the Nation to have a Federal Budget.

If the Tea Party represents fiscal responsibility, its members would necessarily be on record demanding that both the House and Senate Appropriations Committees produce their budget proposals and ensure they are passed and forwarded to the President.

So why is the Nation operating without a Budget?

Why is the Nation funded by Continuing Resolutions?

Why is the Nation *NOT being run as a profitable business?* How can any individual, business, or government bring its deficits under control, when it refuses to generate a budget, and persists in simply spending as if everything were an emergency?

How can a Nation function when its consumers live on the verge of state induced poverty?

Curiously, if the government were to enact anything similar to suggestion made in the previous chapter – provide every working age citizen a poverty level paycheck – the unemployment benefits would be a nonissue, and the nation would not have the deficits or debt associated with ineffective stimulus packages.

Where is the evidence of fiscal responsibility on the part of the Tea Party? Of course they can blame others, but shouldn't they do so with clear evidence in hand that they did their part at every step in the budgetary process?

Whoever is elected in 2014 will need to first contend with the existence, or lack thereof, of a 2014 Federal Budget.

Of course, the immediate problem would be the fact that, for their first term, the President they are contending with would be Obama. Which, in terms of 2016, is actually an ideal situation for those who have constructive reforms designed to limit government and enhance fiscal responsibility.

However, the Tea Party case is seriously threatened by their suggestions that Rafael Edward Cruz is somehow Constitutionally eligible, or qualified, to be considered a presidential candidate.

Ted Cruz was born in Alberta Canada, and is a citizen only because his was a citizen. He is not, as required under Article II, Section 1, a 'natural born citizen' – that is, a citizen by virtue of birth on American soil. The case could be made that the phrase is a reference to having an American mother, but that doesn't fit the context of its origin.

Moreover, if being born in a foreign nation was authorized, then the child of Americans, who was born and raised in a foreign nation, could immigrate at the age of twenty and be qualified to be President when they were thirty-five. That could result in an al-Qaeda raised and trained individual, backed by Middle Eastern oil money, becoming the Commander-in-Chief of the American Armed

Forces, with veto over all legislation and law enforcement powers.

If that is really the long-term risk Americans wish to take, it would be feasible for them to obtain a Supreme Court interpretation which would open the door to that eventuality. But, recent history aside, are Americans that suicidal?

In 2014, 33 of the 100 seats in the United States Senate will come into contention. That's fully one-third of Senatorial power, of that, half are currently in the hands of the 53 member Democratic majority – with two independents who lean Democratic. Therefore, a Tea party slate would only need to win six additional seats.

With control of both the House and Senate, the fact that the President is a Democrat and holds veto power, is irrelevant. In fact, in terms of the 2016 election, it is actually beneficial.

If, instead of taking a nay-sayer position on issues, the Tea Party were to show clear legislative leadership through legislation which clearly serves the interest of the people, while also limiting government intrusion into private lives, it could put forth a winning candidate. But it would require their legislation be forward looking, fiscally responsible, and provide answers to the problems which will confront the next President; if which any Obama veto would serve their needs.

So long as the legislation is clearly presented – none of the "it's bad", or generalized 'we're against', type statements – whoever stands on the Democratic ticket would be faced with the awkward problem of either denouncing a reform which is clearly warranted, or denouncing Obama and any Democrat who opposed the reform.

But that assumes there are rational changes, and that the Tea Party is capable of demonstrating the ability to both recognize them, and provide intelligent solutions.

Simply asserting vague platform statements favoring limited government, free markets, traditional values, enhanced security, while clearly opposing a healthy educated population, is not going to set the stage for public confidence. It will not yield a presidential office, or even carrying a Congressional majority in both Houses.

If anything, a failure to enumerate a clearly positive agenda can only serve to negatively impact both the 2014 and 2016 election results. A fact that remains true, so long as the American voter does not seek to vote against their own long-term best interest.

Personally, the current vocal behavior evidenced across the internet and in the media would tend to argue in favor of a public which hates reality – therefore will weaken the government.

An ongoing problem is the continual use of the word 'reform' as code for eliminate, destroy, impoverish, and facilitate the looting of the American Treasury by the top one percent of the population.

In the name of eliminating government intrusion on the lives of citizens, and the operation of the free market capitalist system, we can 'reform' the tax code – as has been done in the past. That is a nice way of saying we can shift the tax burden on to the middle, and lower middle, class. Ideally, promoters of those reforms are in hopes they will shift the burden to those on the brink of poverty.

Slashing rates to the wealthy is akin to underwriting their lifestyle excesses. The Founding Fathers viewed taxes as a flat rate system which should target the wealthy – at that time, those who owned the plantations and produced the wealth. But Congress has abandoned the fundamental principals which brought the nation into existence. The question now becomes, will the Tea Party Movement continue what Congress started, or will it strive to return to the founding principals?

Will Congress move toward the type of alleged "Entitlement and Pension Reform" which characterized Bush era efforts? Will it seek to privatize Social Security and thereby render it a victim the ups and downs of the stock markets, and thus be easily destroyed by those who promoted policies which caused the 2007 recession?

Will we see the elderly laid victim to a system which is more destructive then the current one – where poverty is assured to any and all who worked diligently, but were unable to save because the private sector investment markets repeatedly collapsed?

Will we privatize Entitlements and slash social programs so that the tax exempt private sector can enhance their cash flow and steal more wealth to be exported to foreign lands?

Will the Congress gain members who realize that the social programs which lift people out of poverty are the same programs which support local supermarkets, and employees, in less populated areas of the nation? Whereas fancy headline grabbing projects only serve to divert resources from where they are most productive.

If a reform were truly a reform, it would enhance the sense of security for citizens, while decreasing the delivery cost of the service or benefit provided.

The idea that we need to 'reform' education should not mean we should promote the teaching of ignorance. But that seems to be what is meant by 'educational reform.' We need to very seriously question why, in 24 of the 50 states, a football coach is paid more than an English teacher – yet hold that English should be our *core language.*

Yes, we can privatize education, but that should mean those schools demonstrate their students routinely excel in the world beyond the classroom. It should not mean we encourage teaching, as fact, alleged 'science' which is demonstrably untrue.

Denial of facts and hypocrisy have become hallmarks of the modern political arena. In that regard, consider the *Birthers* and the attacks on Obama. If he is not Constitutionally qualified by virtue of allegedly being born on foreign soil, why are they quiet about the talk of Ted Cruz running for President?

Moreover, why do the Birthers focus on a birth certificate which is collaborated by a concurrent – Hawaiian Department of Health provided – birth announcement?

Why aren't they going after the mother's passport data; the port of entry immigration records which would demonstrate she was not in the country when he was born? If she was not in Hawaii, obviously he could not have been born there; if she was in Kenya, the British Foreign Office would have a record, and he would, by British law, hold the same status in Britain that Ted Cruz holds in Canada.

But then, if Obama were born in Kenya, by the virtue of his mother's citizenship, he would still be as eligible to hold the highest office in the land as Rafael Edward 'Ted' Cruz is claimed to be.

It would seemingly appear that irrationality and dishonesty are hallmarks of those who would deceive their fellow Americans.

All too often, those promoting the reforms are those whose wealth and position are derived from conning those who buy into the Biblical Literalist-Creationist ideological mindset.

They are, like the Birthers, targeting those who demonstrate the ignorance and superstition which brought about the 'Dark Ages' and exposed Europe to the ravages of plagues and the practice of witch-hunts which ultimately saw the healthy burnt alive because they engaged in simple hygiene, or understood basic pharmacology.

Literalist-Creationist are individuals who basically believe we are all descended from eight people – Noah, his wife, their three sons and the son's wives – who survived a global flood some 4000 years-ago.

They also believe that our Common Calendar (which was created 530 plus years after the historic event) marks the birth of Jesus, when, in fact (as explained in my book Genesis of Genesis) it actually originated when a Scythian Monk simply reset a Metonic node in the Hebrew Calendar to one; thereby fulfilling a papal request to make Easter and Passover coincide in a predictable way.

Those who assert Creationism do not know our New Year's Day was established to mark the eighth day after Christmas – the day Jesus would have been circumcised – and that Christmas is actually the Roman gift giving holiday of Saturnalia which shows reverence to a pagan deity. Big money profits from their ignorance.

The Tea Party recognizes that American politics is burdened by big money from lobbyists and special interests with an undue influence on the peoples' representatives. But, it has been said that Tea Party Republicans speak less for Wall Street than they do for a seething resentment among a poorly educated – if that is so, then the Tea Party is targeting those who lack the intellect to govern. I would hope that is not true. But I must, given the evidence of October 2013, and its supports of the SPARKY1845 ilk, fear that it is.

Consider the membership mentality: Biblical Literalists, are 37% of the Tea Party membership, but only 30% of the American population; as with the general population, slightly more than half believe the Bible to be divinely inspired.

Less than 7% of Tea Party supporters accept that the Bible contains the accumulated knowledge of generations of men devoted to both the acquisition of wisdom and an understanding of the universe we live in.

What we can see as scary about that low level of belief in the Biblical assertion of "Wisdom, Knowledge and Understanding" to be three parts of the divine spirit – so it follows that humans would seek to acquire those things.

(Which opens us to an Eve and Apple debate which has the Tree and Serpent as tools in a divine setup, an effort to make all the scientific and moral knowledge of humans acquire into something more important then everyday survival skills. Something willfully rejected by those who value ignorance and deceit.)

When confronted, with the existence of different races and DNA – which either evolved over tens of thousands of years, or evolved from the Ark's eight human occupants, within 4000 years of recorded history – promoters of literalism modify their logic to both profess that the Biblical calendar is wrong, thus is not literal, and yet it is still to be taken literally. They know the contradiction is beyond the comprehension of their followers, and that they are, in effect admitting to promoting a deceiver deity, or deceiving their followers.

Yet these individuals are the forefront of the attack on the public school system; they want to reform, privatize, the system to allow corporate "entrepreneurs" and profiteers to receive free reign in preparing America's children for a place in the global economy – a place where their intellectual competitors are those who assume roles of Islamic suicide bombers.

When members of Congress speak of 'reform,' who is really speaking for the health and longevity of American society? Is it the Tea Party Movement, or those who serves the great deceiver?

Trickle Down Reality

Shareholder activism, combined with lawsuits sympathetic to shareholder interests, and normal, traditional, corporate board policies in publicly-held companies – where net wealth is related to their stock options – results in the goal of maximizing stock prices.

As a result, corporate attention is focused on short-term stock price and shareholder value considerations – at a cost to the long-term value of employees.

The concept of "trickle down" runs headlong and directly into the concept of short-term inflation of stock value. If you decrease expenses, and are able to maintain constant or growing sales so as to sustain a constant price-earnings ratio, the result is an increase in stock price per share.

Thus there is an economic incentive to – as Pope Francis put it – to increase the size of the glass as the water approaches the top. To continue the Pope's analogy, eventually there is no glass; it is a process which undermines the longevity of the company.

When wage levels are insufficient to afford to feed a single-income family of four, the result is SNAP qualification – the family goes on Food Stamps, and possibly qualifies for a wide range of other governmental benefits, or entitlements.

Under current (2013) law, to qualify, the family would need an income that is less than $2500 per month, which, for a 40 hour work week, is equivalent to $15 per hour. Since 24 July 2009, the Federal minimum wage has been $7.25 per hour – or less than half of what the family needs just to survive.

(See page 106 for table of Minimum Wages by State)

Simple math which underscores a problem characterized by Birther logic and manifested in routine assertions about families on welfare not wanting to work – when the reality demonstrates that two parents, each working at a minimum wage job, still can not achieve the minimum income to sustain two children. Though they would have enough to raise one child.

Consolidated State Minimum Wage Table

Alabama: $7.25	Montana: $7.90
Alaska: $7.75	Nebraska: $7.25
Arizona: $7.90	New Hampshire: $7.25
Arkansas: $7.25	New Jersey: $8.25
Colorado: $8.00	North Carolina: $7.25
Delaware: $7.25	North Dakota: $7.25
Florida: $7.93	Ohio: $7.95
Georgia: $7.25	Oklahoma: $7.25
Hawaii: $7.25	Oregon: $9.10
Idaho: $7.25	Pennsylvania: $7.25
Illinois: $8.25	Puerto Rico: $7.25
Indiana: $7.25	Rhode Island: $8.00
Iowa: $7.25	South Carolina: $7.25
Kansas: $7.25	South Dakota: $7.25
Kentucky: $7.25	Tennessee: $7.25
Louisiana: $7.25	Texas: $7.25
Maine: $7.50	Utah: $7.25
Maryland: $7.25	Virginia: $7.25
Massachusetts: $8.00	Vermont: $8.73
Michigan: $7.40	Washington: $9.32
Minnesota: $6.15	West Virginia: $7.25
Missouri: $7.50	Wisconsin: $7.25
Mississippi: $7.25	Wyoming: $7.25

New Mexico: $7.50
            - Albuquerque: $8.60

California: $8.00
            - San Francisco: $10.74
                        - San Jose: $10.15
(increase to $9.00 on July 1, 2014 and $10.00 on January 1, 2016)
Connecticut: $8.70
($9.00 effective January 1, 2015)
Nevada:
$7.25 for employees who receive qualifying health benefits,
$8.25 for employees who do not receive qualifying health benefits.
New York: $8.00
($8.75 on December 31, 2014, $9.00 on December 31, 2015)

If a condom broke, diaphragm shifted, or the pill failed to do its job, Right-to-Life groups would ignore the realities and insist the child be born, even if if the parents recognized the realities and opted for abortion. Within certain segments of society, there seems to be a deep seated desire to plunge people into poverty, then belittle them for being poor, and subsequently cut assistance. It is the moral core of a powerful segment of American society.

As tabulated, effective 2013, five states effectively have not set their own minimum; four are below the federal level; twenty-two affirmed the federal minimum; and nineteen states have minimums which are set above the federal level – the highest minimum, $9.19 per hour, was in the State of Washington. But, in December 2013, that changed when the District of Columbia voted to gradually raise its minimum wage to $11.50 per hour by 2016. Prior to the DC City Council vote, other cities and states had also begun to raise their minimum wages. The city of SeaTac, Washington brought its wage to the necessary $15 per hour.

Effectively, all minimum wage laws are geared to ensure that qualify for government assistance. Accordingly, wages are set to a those in a single wage earner family, of two or more members, will standard that maximizes shareholder stock prices without imposing a need for corporate efficiency.

As a theory, and as a reality, does trickle down make sense?

If we look to an analogy, we can see learn the benefit and the pitfalls of the Trickle Down theory.

Consider a house. For the sake of this example, make it an old new England Cap Code, its roof sloped about forty-five degrees from peak to front and rear.

A light rain falls and quickly trickles down old cedar shingles to an edge which may, or may not, have a gutter carved of a single piece of cedar hone from one of many cedar trees growing among the New England pines and spruce.

If there is a gutter, the rain is captured and guided to a down spout, and there, through a pounded metal tube to be collected in a rain barrel, or guided into a stone, or concrete cistern in the cellar.

Regardless of how the water is captured, it can be captured soa manner which will allow it to be used – the home has no well, no source of running water, just buckets which will bring and hold the water from the barrel, or a hand-pump which will raise the water from cistern to sink.

Regardless of the means by which it enters the home, it does so in a controlled manner and is then utilized for cooking, washing and drinking. From random rain and its trickle down, each step is under human control and guidance – nobody would expect a simple roof to deliver the water to the proper place within the home, or make it available when and where it is needed. The water requires a secondary guidance system.

Remove the finely crafted cedar gutters, allow the roof the freedom to handle the trickle down it is charged with creating and the water will still flow downward. When it hits the edge of the roof, it will continue to flow in the same downward path to the ground.

If the rain is heavy, the flow will be fast, and the water will pour off to soak the ground along the foundation.

If the rain is gentle, when the flow reaches the edge, it will follow around to the fascia board and continue to cling to the house, as it moves down the clapboard or shingled walls – seeking refuge in any gap, or crack, and puddling in any space which might give it refuge.

The puddles behind the shingle or clapboard will soak in, as will the streams which rounded the fascia, and with time the wood will soften, rot and fall away. The weakened structure of the house will eventually yield to its own weight and the combined forces of nature to collapse into a useless pile of rubble.

The water which flowed freely in torrents from the roof, the water which soaked into the ground, will find refuge until a time of frost, when it will freeze and expand. That expansion will push outward against the frozen ground, and inward against the surface of the home's foundation – a foundation which defines the cellar, a places of emptiness offering no resistance to the pressure.

As a result, long after the trickle down, cracks form in the foundation. Or water might soak down far enough to soften the ground beneath the footings and the house will shift as it settles into the wet soil – becoming like the Leaning Tower of Pisa. But, not designed for an imbalanced posture, the frame will twist, plaster will crack and eventually, even if the structure does not fall, it will become uninhabitable.

These are the realities of planed and unplanned trickle down.

If we consider it in terms of economic theory, the effects are the same. The only differences are that we are discussing money instead of water, and people's lives instead of structures.

If we guide the flow of cash from the rich to the poor, it can be used productively. Allowed to flow unguided, ultimately, with the passage of time and natural variants in economic forces – like the seasonal variants of nature – the unregulated trickle becomes a destructive force which, ultimately, brings down the economy by destroying the people and families which are its core structure and foundation.

What damage does a below poverty level minim wage create for society? The most obvious problem is one of subsidies.

For people to live and work, they must be able to eat, have a place to live, and be in reasonably good health – a sick worker is an unproductive worker. And a worker who is concerned about a sick spouse, or child, is one who will be distracted from their job.

Like water running down the side of the house, detractions may seem inconsequential, might even go unnoticed – right up until that mistake, or accident, which disrupts production, or creates an "accounting error" which ultimately costs the firm thousands, or even millions. Distractions are stress, as with structural stress, one might not be meaningful, but multiple, coming at the right time, are the basis of the "Straw which broke the camel's back."

It only takes one 'bad' decision, at a critical juncture in the decision, or policy, making process – the foundation will crack, the movement will cause a domino effect, and the nation falls into a recession, or even a major depression.

It might be as simple as playing brinkmanship with the full

faith and credit of the American government – as simple as failing to pass a budget, or voting to default on the lawful obligations that are represented by our National Debt.

It begins with a small crack. It begins with a shadow query as to whether or not, at some time in the future, a vote to default will carry, and whether or not there is some alternative safe-haven currency, an alternative to the American Dollar.

Having seen the crack, but not its repair, and with the effect of Greek bankruptcy still reverberating throughout the European Union, at some point a major creditor will make the decision to seek another repository. If that decision coincides with a critical time in history, the American house will shift on its foundation.

The vague, but meaningful, Tea Party principals and core beliefs are the strengths and weaknesses of the American structure and its foundation.

We can allow our financial waters to trickle down – and do their damage – or we can guide them to places where they can be used to nurture the economy. The difference might be a function of intent, or one of unintended consequences.

We have seen, and are witnessing, the effect of the Law of Unintended Consequences in the interaction between the 'Right-to-Life' movement and the 'Defense of Marriage' Act.

Regardless of marital status, 'Right-to-Life' demands that a fetus become a child.

'Defense of Marriage' strived to deny the right of marriage to couples who have spent decades in a 'forbidden' loving relationship. A relationship which was forbidden without any real justification, or meaning. At best it served only to deny the right of benefits, or statutory rights of inheritance – with no redeeming social benefit.

When people looked at the reality of modern marriage, they saw a culture which practiced serial-monogamy. A culture where half of all marriages ended in divorce and respected public figures often had two or more marriages to their credit.

As a result, the two movements came together to declare that marriage was not necessary for procreation, and was not valued by the culture.

While 'Right-to-Life' groups demanded the birth of a child, but they did nothing to promote adoption. Accordingly, those who wanted children often ventured overseas to find what was denied them in their own country. Once again public figures adopting one or more children from third world countries – often with a partner to whom they are not married.

A Pew Research Center survey, indicated half of Americans now believe co-habitation to be acceptable, while 38 percent are still of the opinion that living together is bad for society. However, one need only consider Thomas Jefferson and his sister-in-law, Sarah Hemings, to realize that co-habitation has a long history in America, as well as the world. That it could also produces children while being socially frowned upon is also one of our 'traditional values.'

A the Centers for Disease Control and Prevention found that unmarried couples living together account for 22 percent, or nearly one in four, first-born babies. That number is up from 12 percent in 2002, and reflects a rapid growth since the 1996 passage of the 'Defense of Marriage Act' discredited marriage's true significance – a legal social bond between loving individuals.

Traditionally, men and women of lower education levels have more children than those who attended college; they were also more likely to have them out of wedlock – that seems to be changing.

We appear to be at an interesting point in history. Many of the old superstitions and pagan impositions of European religion are in the process of being dispensed with. At the same time, the global economy is creating pressures for change which threatens to reveal the full extent to which many within once dominant nations are on the verge of poverty and economic disaster.

In America, an estimated 42 million women, and 28 million children are faced with financial hardship which could easily be alleviated by a fiscally rational Congress.

If we consider that women earn the majority of secondary degrees, and represent more than half of the country's voters, they still comprise close to two-thirds of minimum-wage workers.

Part of that problem is that they are expected to do it all – be workers, parents and care-givers. But because woman occupy so many minimum wage positions which ensure poverty, the average earnings of full-time female worker is now 80.9 percent of average male earnings. (up from 77 percent; and by age, 93 percent.)

The court system is geared to placing children into maternal care and custody situations, with the result that 40 percent of all American households with children below voting age have the mother as either the only or primary income provider. Note the term 'primary'. The fact that minimum wages range from two-thirds to half of poverty level, and have no paid sick days, even assuming reasonable child support payments, there is insufficient funds to lift many above the poverty level.

This matter is complicated by the fact that many Entitlement programs effectively confiscate the support payments to offset the entitlement outlays. Thus, millions of women are still struggling on societal margins because the governmental programs and the courts are tailored to keep them there.

If we look to Third World nations and those regions where Sharia Law prevails, we quickly see that by leaving women out of the mainstream denies a nation and a region the benefits of a full and robust economy.

These are factors which the Tea Party Movement must take into consideration when structuring the legislation to support tits stated beliefs and objectives.

Unfortunately, many of the most serious problems have been introduced by, or emerge from, positions of the political party with which it has aligned itself.

To know the position that party will adopt, one need only ask: What, over the long-term, will inflict the most harm to the most people? Answer that question honestly, and free from the historic bigotry and irrationality of social suppression, and you will always know the way a third will vote. Add in the politics of their financial constituents – who always focus on short-term outcomes – and you have the totality of their vote.